C# AND ODBC

Working with the Dataview

Richard Thomas Edwards

CONTENTS

WHY IS THE CODE BROKEN INTO SECTIONS?...4

A lot of code to cover 10

    Connection, Command and DataAdapter..10

    Connection and DataAdapter 11

    Command and DataAdapter 11

    DataAdapter 11

    DataTable 11

ASP Examples 12

    HORIZONTAL 12

    VERTICAL 16

ASPX Examples 20

    HORIZONTAL...20

    VERTICAL...24

HTA Examples...27

    HORIZONTAL...27

    VERTICAL 31

HTA Examples...35

    HORIZONTAL...35

    VERTICAL...39

Delimited Text Files 43

    COLON DELIMITED HORIZONTAL VIEW..43

    COLON DELIMITED VERTICAL VIEW 44

    COMMA DELIMITED HORIZONTAL VIEW......................................44

    COMMA DELIMITED VERTICAL VIEW...45

    EXCLAMATION DELIMITED HORIZONTAL VIEW 46

EXCLAMATION DELIMITED VERTICAL VIEW 46

SEMI-COLON DELIMITED HORIZONTAL VIEW 47

SEMI-COLON DELIMITED VERTICAL VIEW 48

TAB DELIMITED HORIZONTAL VIEW 48

TAB DELIMITED VERTICAL VIEW 49

TILDE DELIMITED HORIZONTAL VIEW...49

TILDE DELIMITED VERTICAL VIEW 50

Working Excel 52

HORIZONTAL AUTOMATION 52

VERTICAL AUTOMATION 53

SPREADSHEET...53

HORIZONTAL CSV 55

VERTICAL CSV 56

XML Files...57

TEXT CREATED ATTRIBUTE XML...57

DOM CREATED ATTRIBUTE XML..58

TEXT CREATED ELEMENT XML...59

DOM CREATE ELEMENT XML 59

TEXT CREATED ELEMENT XML FOR XLS...60

DOM CREATE ELEMENT XML FOR XSL 60

TEXT CREATED SCHEMA XML 61

DOM CREATED SCHEMA XML..62

XSL Files..63

Single Line Horizontal 64

Multi Line Horizontal..67

Single Line VERTICAL...70

Multi Line VERTICAL 72

StYlesheets 75

WHY IS THE CODE
BROKEN INTO
SECTIONS?

This book is really condensed

THIS BOOK IS REALL A HUGE BOOK! It just doesn't look that way if you're looking at just the length of it. For example, if you were to eliminate the stylesheets, there are approximately 68 pages before I added one – just one – example of a complete code example. In-other-words, 6 pages of one code example is almost 10 percent of this book. Imagine what 5760 would look like at just 5 pages each! This book would wind up being 28800 pages in length.

Yet, it is, indeed, all here!

```
string cnstr = "Driver={Microsoft Access Driver (*.mdb)};DBQ=C:\NWIND.MDB";
string strQuery = "Select * From [Products]";

System.Data.ODBC.ODBCConnection cn = new
System.Data.ODBC.ODBCConnection(cnstr);
cn.Open();

System.Data.ODBC.ODBCCommand cmd = new System.Data.ODBC.ODBCCommand();
cmd.Connection = cn;
cmd.CommandType = 1;
cmd.CommandText = strQuery;
cmd.ExecuteNonquery();
```

```
System.Data.ODBC.ODBCDataAdapter da = new
System.Data.ODBC.ODBCDataAdapter(cmd);

System.Data.DataTable dt as new System.Data.DataTable();
da.Fill(dt);
System.Data.DataView dv = dv.Table.DefaultView;
Scripting.FileSystemObject fso = new Scripting.FileSystemObject();
Scripting.TextStream txtstream = fso.OpenTextFile(Application.StartupPath +
"\\Products.html",IOMode.ForWriting, True, Tristate.TristateUseDefault);
txtstream.WriteLine("<html>");
txtstream.WriteLine("<head>");
txtstream.WriteLine("<title>Products</title>");
txtstream.WriteLine("<style type='text/css'>");
txtstream.WriteLine("body");
txtstream.WriteLine("{");
txtstream.WriteLine("   PADDING-RIGHT: 0px;");
txtstream.WriteLine("   PADDING-LEFT: 0px;");
txtstream.WriteLine("   PADDING-BOTTOM: 0px;");
txtstream.WriteLine("   MARGIN: 0px;");
txtstream.WriteLine("   COLOR: #333;");
txtstream.WriteLine("   PADDING-TOP: 0px;");
txtstream.WriteLine("   FONT-FAMILY: verdana, arial, helvetica, sans-serif;");
txtstream.WriteLine("}");
txtstream.WriteLine("table");
txtstream.WriteLine("{");
txtstream.WriteLine("   BORDER-RIGHT: #999999 1px solid;");
txtstream.WriteLine("   PADDING-RIGHT: 1px;");
txtstream.WriteLine("   PADDING-LEFT: 1px;");
txtstream.WriteLine("   PADDING-BOTTOM: 1px;");
txtstream.WriteLine("   LINE-HEIGHT: 8px;");
txtstream.WriteLine("   PADDING-TOP: 1px;");
txtstream.WriteLine("   BORDER-BOTTOM: #999 1px solid;");
txtstream.WriteLine("   BACKGROUND-COLOR: #eeeeee;");
txtstream.WriteLine("
filter:progid:DXImageTransform.Microsoft.Shadow(color='silver', Direction=135,
Strength=16)");
txtstream.WriteLine("}");
txtstream.WriteLine("th");
txtstream.WriteLine("{");
txtstream.WriteLine("   BORDER-RIGHT: #999999 3px solid;");
txtstream.WriteLine("   PADDING-RIGHT: 6px;");
txtstream.WriteLine("   PADDING-LEFT: 6px;");
txtstream.WriteLine("   FONT-WEIGHT: Bold;");
txtstream.WriteLine("   FONT-SIZE: 14px;");
txtstream.WriteLine("   PADDING-BOTTOM: 6px;");
txtstream.WriteLine("   COLOR: darkred;");
txtstream.WriteLine("   LINE-HEIGHT: 14px;");
txtstream.WriteLine("   PADDING-TOP: 6px;");
txtstream.WriteLine("   BORDER-BOTTOM: #999 1px solid;");
txtstream.WriteLine("   BACKGROUND-COLOR: #eeeeee;");
```

```
txtstream.WriteLine("    FONT-FAMILY: font-family: Cambria, serif;");
txtstream.WriteLine("    FONT-SIZE: 12px;");
txtstream.WriteLine("    text-align: left;");
txtstream.WriteLine("    white-Space: nowrap='nowrap';");
txtstream.WriteLine("}");
txtstream.WriteLine(".th");
txtstream.WriteLine("{");
txtstream.WriteLine("    BORDER-RIGHT: #999999 2px solid;");
txtstream.WriteLine("    PADDING-RIGHT: 6px;");
txtstream.WriteLine("    PADDING-LEFT: 6px;");
txtstream.WriteLine("    FONT-WEIGHT: Bold;");
txtstream.WriteLine("    PADDING-BOTTOM: 6px;");
txtstream.WriteLine("    COLOR: black;");
txtstream.WriteLine("    PADDING-TOP: 6px;");
txtstream.WriteLine("    BORDER-BOTTOM: #999 2px solid;");
txtstream.WriteLine("    BACKGROUND-COLOR: #eeeeee;");
txtstream.WriteLine("    FONT-FAMILY: font-family: Cambria, serif;");
txtstream.WriteLine("    FONT-SIZE: 10px;");
txtstream.WriteLine("    text-align: right;");
txtstream.WriteLine("    white-Space: nowrap='nowrap';");
txtstream.WriteLine("}");
txtstream.WriteLine("td");
txtstream.WriteLine("{");
txtstream.WriteLine("    BORDER-RIGHT: #999999 3px solid;");
txtstream.WriteLine("    PADDING-RIGHT: 6px;");
txtstream.WriteLine("    PADDING-LEFT: 6px;");
txtstream.WriteLine("    FONT-WEIGHT: Normal;");
txtstream.WriteLine("    PADDING-BOTTOM: 6px;");
txtstream.WriteLine("    COLOR: navy;");
txtstream.WriteLine("    LINE-HEIGHT: 14px;");
txtstream.WriteLine("    PADDING-TOP: 6px;");
txtstream.WriteLine("    BORDER-BOTTOM: #999 1px solid;");
txtstream.WriteLine("    BACKGROUND-COLOR: #eeeeee;");
txtstream.WriteLine("    FONT-FAMILY: font-family: Cambria, serif;");
txtstream.WriteLine("    FONT-SIZE: 12px;");
txtstream.WriteLine("    text-align: left;");
txtstream.WriteLine("    white-Space: nowrap='nowrap';");
txtstream.WriteLine("}");
txtstream.WriteLine("div");
txtstream.WriteLine("{");
txtstream.WriteLine("    BORDER-RIGHT: #999999 3px solid;");
txtstream.WriteLine("    PADDING-RIGHT: 6px;");
txtstream.WriteLine("    PADDING-LEFT: 6px;");
txtstream.WriteLine("    FONT-WEIGHT: Normal;");
txtstream.WriteLine("    PADDING-BOTTOM: 6px;");
txtstream.WriteLine("    COLOR: white;");
txtstream.WriteLine("    PADDING-TOP: 6px;");
txtstream.WriteLine("    BORDER-BOTTOM: #999 1px solid;");
txtstream.WriteLine("    BACKGROUND-COLOR: navy;");
txtstream.WriteLine("    FONT-FAMILY: font-family: Cambria, serif;");
```

```
txtstream.WriteLine("    FONT-SIZE: 10px;");
txtstream.WriteLine("    text-align: left;");
txtstream.WriteLine("    white-Space: nowrap='nowrap';");
txtstream.WriteLine("}");
txtstream.WriteLine("span");
txtstream.WriteLine("{");
txtstream.WriteLine("    BORDER-RIGHT: #999999 3px solid;");
txtstream.WriteLine("    PADDING-RIGHT: 3px;");
txtstream.WriteLine("    PADDING-LEFT: 3px;");
txtstream.WriteLine("    FONT-WEIGHT: Normal;");
txtstream.WriteLine("    PADDING-BOTTOM: 3px;");
txtstream.WriteLine("    COLOR: white;");
txtstream.WriteLine("    PADDING-TOP: 3px;");
txtstream.WriteLine("    BORDER-BOTTOM: #999 1px solid;");
txtstream.WriteLine("    BACKGROUND-COLOR: navy;");
txtstream.WriteLine("    FONT-FAMILY: font-family: Cambria, serif;");
txtstream.WriteLine("    FONT-SIZE: 10px;");
txtstream.WriteLine("    text-align: left;");
txtstream.WriteLine("    white-Space: nowrap='nowrap';");
txtstream.WriteLine("    display: inline-block;");
txtstream.WriteLine("    width: 100%;");
txtstream.WriteLine("}");
txtstream.WriteLine("textarea");
txtstream.WriteLine("{");
txtstream.WriteLine("    BORDER-RIGHT: #999999 3px solid;");
txtstream.WriteLine("    PADDING-RIGHT: 3px;");
txtstream.WriteLine("    PADDING-LEFT: 3px;");
txtstream.WriteLine("    FONT-WEIGHT: Normal;");
txtstream.WriteLine("    PADDING-BOTTOM: 3px;");
txtstream.WriteLine("    COLOR: white;");
txtstream.WriteLine("    PADDING-TOP: 3px;");
txtstream.WriteLine("    BORDER-BOTTOM: #999 1px solid;");
txtstream.WriteLine("    BACKGROUND-COLOR: navy;");
txtstream.WriteLine("    FONT-FAMILY: font-family: Cambria, serif;");
txtstream.WriteLine("    FONT-SIZE: 10px;");
txtstream.WriteLine("    text-align: left;");
txtstream.WriteLine("    white-Space: nowrap='nowrap';");
txtstream.WriteLine("    width: 100%;");
txtstream.WriteLine("}");
txtstream.WriteLine("select");
txtstream.WriteLine("{");
txtstream.WriteLine("    BORDER-RIGHT: #999999 3px solid;");
txtstream.WriteLine("    PADDING-RIGHT: 6px;");
txtstream.WriteLine("    PADDING-LEFT: 6px;");
txtstream.WriteLine("    FONT-WEIGHT: Normal;");
txtstream.WriteLine("    PADDING-BOTTOM: 6px;");
txtstream.WriteLine("    COLOR: white;");
txtstream.WriteLine("    PADDING-TOP: 6px;");
txtstream.WriteLine("    BORDER-BOTTOM: #999 1px solid;");
txtstream.WriteLine("    BACKGROUND-COLOR: navy;");
```

```
txtstream.WriteLine("    FONT-FAMILY: font-family: Cambria, serif;");
txtstream.WriteLine("    FONT-SIZE: 10px;");
txtstream.WriteLine("    text-align: left;");
txtstream.WriteLine("    white-Space: nowrap='nowrap';");
txtstream.WriteLine("    width: 100%;");
txtstream.WriteLine("}");
txtstream.WriteLine("input");
txtstream.WriteLine("{");
txtstream.WriteLine("    BORDER-RIGHT: #999999 3px solid;");
txtstream.WriteLine("    PADDING-RIGHT: 3px;");
txtstream.WriteLine("    PADDING-LEFT: 3px;");
txtstream.WriteLine("    FONT-WEIGHT: Bold;");
txtstream.WriteLine("    PADDING-BOTTOM: 3px;");
txtstream.WriteLine("    COLOR: white;");
txtstream.WriteLine("    PADDING-TOP: 3px;");
txtstream.WriteLine("    BORDER-BOTTOM: #999 1px solid;");
txtstream.WriteLine("    BACKGROUND-COLOR: navy;");
txtstream.WriteLine("    FONT-FAMILY: font-family: Cambria, serif;");
txtstream.WriteLine("    FONT-SIZE: 12px;");
txtstream.WriteLine("    text-align: left;");
txtstream.WriteLine("    display: table-cell;");
txtstream.WriteLine("    white-Space: nowrap='nowrap';");
txtstream.WriteLine("    width: 100%;");
txtstream.WriteLine("}");
txtstream.WriteLine("h1 {");
txtstream.WriteLine("color: antiquewhite;");
txtstream.WriteLine("text-shadow: 1px 1px 1px black;");
txtstream.WriteLine("padding: 3px;");
txtstream.WriteLine("text-align: center;");
txtstream.WriteLine("box-shadow: inset 2px 2px 5px rgba(0,0,0,0.5), inset -2px -
2px 5px rgba(255,255,255,0.5);");
txtstream.WriteLine("}");
txtstream.WriteLine("</style>");
txtstream.WriteLine("<body>");
txtstream.WriteLine("<center>");
txtstream.WriteLine("</br>");
txtstream.WriteLine("</br>");
txtstream.WriteLine("<table border=0 cellspacing=3 cellpadding=3");
txtstream.WriteLine("<tr>");
foreach col as System.Data.DataColumn in ds.Tables(0).Columns
{
    txtstream.WriteLine("<th align='left' nowrap='nowrap'>" + col.Caption +
"</th>");
}
txtstream.WriteLine("</tr>");

foreach row as System.Data.DataRow in ds.Tables(0).Rows)
{
    txtstream.WriteLine("<tr>");
    foreach col as System.Data.DataColumn in ds.Tables(0).Columns
```

```
    {
        txtstream.WriteLine("<td  align='left' nowrap='true'><input type=text
value="""" + row[col.Caption].ToString() + """"></input></td>");
    }
    txtstream.WriteLine("</tr>");
}
txtstream.WriteLine("</table>");
txtstream.WriteLine("</body>");
txtstream.WriteLine("</html>");
txtstream.Close();
```

A LOT OF CODE TO
COVER

Overview

T HERE IS A LOT OF CODE TO COVER AND, HONESTLY, I HATE INTRODUCTIONS. So, let's make this short and sweet. We're using ODBC and the DataTable to create outputs that include ASP, ASPX, Delimited Text Files, Excel, HTA, HTML, XML, and XSL. There, I said it, I'm done.

From the ODBC Coding perspective, use the following:

```
string cnstr = "";
string strQuery = "";
```

Connection, Command and DataAdapter

```
System.Data.ODBC.ODBCConnection cn = new
System.Data.ODBC.ODBCConnection(cnstr);
cn.Open();

System.Data.ODBC.ODBCCommand cmd = new
System.Data.ODBC.ODBCCommand();
```

```
cmd.Connection = cn;"
cmd.CommandType = 1;
cmd.CommandText = strQuery;
cmd.ExecuteNonquery();

System.Data.ODBC.ODBCDataAdapter da = new
System.Data.ODBC.ODBCDataAdapter(cmd);
```

Connection and DataAdapter

```
System.Data.ODBC.ODBCConnection cn = new
System.Data.ODBC.ODBCConnection(cnstr);
cn.Open();

System.Data.ODBC.ODBCDataAdapter da = new
System.Data.ODBC.ODBCDataAdapter(strQuery, cn);
```

Command and DataAdapter

```
System.Data.ODBC.ODBCCommand cmd = new
System.Data.ODBC.ODBCCommand();
cmd.Connection = new System.Data.ODBC.ODBCConnection;"
cmd.Connection.ConnectionString = cnstr;")
cmd.Connection.Open();

cmd.CommandType = 1;
cmd.CommandText = strQuery;
cmd.ExecuteNonQuery();

System.Data.ODBC.ODBCDataAdapter da = new
System.Data.ODBC.ODBCDataAdapter(cmd);
```

DataAdapter

```
System.Data.ODBC.ODBCDataAdapter da = new
System.Data.ODBC.ODBCDataAdapter(strQuery, cnstr);
```

DataTable

```
System.Data.DataTable dt  = new System.Data.DataTable;
da.Fill(dt);
System.Data.DataView dv = dv.Table.DefaultView;
```

You are going to need to add this to the routines to the code below because they and some additional code logic takes up way too many pages.

ASP EXAMPLES

Let's do it!

Below, are examples of using ODBC, the DataTable and ASP. And just in case you are wondering, I use none as meaning no additional tags between the <td></td>

HORIZONTAL

```
Scripting.FileSystemObject fso = new Scripting.FileSystemObject();
Scripting.TextStream txtstream = fso.OpenTextFile(Application.StartupPath +
"\\Products.asp",IOMode.ForWriting, True, Tristate.TristateUseDefault);
txtstream.WriteLine("<html>");
txtstream.WriteLine("<head>");
txtstream.WriteLine("<title>Products</title>");
txtstream.WriteLine("<body>");
```

For Reports:

```
txtstream.WriteLine("<table border=0 cellspacing=3 cellpadding=3>");
```

For Tables:

```
txtstream.WriteLine("<table border=1 cellspacing=3 cellpadding=3>");

txtstream.WriteLine("<%");
txtstream.WriteLine("Response.Write(""<tr>"" & vbcrlf)");
foreach(System.Data.DataColumn col in dv.Table.Columns)
{
```

```
    txtstream.WriteLine("Response.Write(""""<th align='left' nowrap='nowrap'>" +
col.Caption + "</th>"""" & vbcrlf)");
    }
    txtstream.WriteLine("Response.Write(""""</tr>"""" & vbcrlf)");
```

Additional Tags:

None

```
    foreach(System.Data.DataRow row in dv.Table.Rows)
    {
        txtstream.WriteLine("Response.Write(""""<tr>"""" & vbcrlf)");
        foreach(System.Data.DataColumn col in dv.Table.Columns)
        {
            txtstream.WriteLine("Response.Write(""""<td  align='left' nowrap='nowrap'>"
+ row[col.Caption].ToString() + "</td>"""" & vbcrlf)");
        }
        txtstream.WriteLine("Response.Write(""""</tr>"""" & vbcrlf)");
    }
```

Button

```
    foreach(System.Data.DataRow row in dv.Table.Rows)
    {
        txtstream.WriteLine("Response.Write(""""<tr>"""" & vbcrlf)");
        foreach(System.Data.DataColumn col in dv.Table.Columns)
        {
            txtstream.WriteLine("Response.Write(""""<td  align='left'
nowrap='true'><button style='width:100%;' value ='" + row[col.Caption].ToString()
+ "'>" + row[col.Caption].ToString() + "</button></td>"""" & vbcrlf)");
        }
        txtstream.WriteLine("Response.Write(""""</tr>"""" & vbcrlf)");
    }
```

Combobox

```
    foreach(System.Data.DataRow row in dv.Table.Rows)
    {
        txtstream.WriteLine("Response.Write(""""<tr>"""" & vbcrlf)");
        foreach(System.Data.DataColumn col in dv.Table.Columns)
        {
            txtstream.WriteLine("Response.Write(""""<td  align='left'
nowrap='true'><select><option value = """" + row[col.Caption].ToString() + """">" +
row[col.Caption].ToString() + "</option></select></td>"""" & vbcrlf)");
        }
        txtstream.WriteLine("Response.Write(""""</tr>"""" & vbcrlf)");
    }
```

Div

```
foreach(System.Data.DataRow row in dv.Table.Rows)
{
    txtstream.WriteLine("Response.Write(""<tr>""" & vbcrlf)");
    foreach(System.Data.DataColumn col in dv.Table.Columns)
    {
        txtstream.WriteLine("Response.Write(""<td  align='left'
nowrap='true'><div>" + row[col.Caption].ToString() + "</div></td>""" & vbcrlf)");
    }
    txtstream.WriteLine("Response.Write(""</tr>""" & vbcrlf)");
}
```

Link

```
foreach(System.Data.DataRow row in dv.Table.Rows)
{
    txtstream.WriteLine("Response.Write(""<tr>""" & vbcrlf)");
    foreach(System.Data.DataColumn col in dv.Table.Columns)
    {
        txtstream.WriteLine("Response.Write(""<td  align='left' nowrap='true'><a
href='" + row[col.Caption].ToString() + "'>" + row[col.Caption].ToString() +
"</a></td>""" & vbcrlf)");
    }
    txtstream.WriteLine("Response.Write(""</tr>""" & vbcrlf)");
}
```

Listbox

```
foreach(System.Data.DataRow row in dv.Table.Rows)
{
    txtstream.WriteLine("Response.Write(""<tr>""" & vbcrlf)");
    foreach(System.Data.DataColumn col in dv.Table.Columns)
    {
        txtstream.WriteLine("Response.Write(""<td  align='left'
nowrap='true'><select multiple><option value = """" + row[col.Caption].ToString() +
"""">" + row[col.Caption].ToString() + "</option></select></td>""" & vbcrlf)");
    }
    txtstream.WriteLine("Response.Write(""</tr>""" & vbcrlf)");
}
```

Span

```
foreach(System.Data.DataRow row in dv.Table.Rows)
{
```

```
    txtstream.WriteLine("Response.Write(""<tr>"" & vbcrlf)");
    foreach(System.Data.DataColumn col in dv.Table.Columns)
    {
        txtstream.WriteLine("Response.Write(""<td  align='left'
nowrap='true'><span>" + row[col.Caption].ToString() + "</span></td>"" &
vbcrlf)");
    }
    txtstream.WriteLine("Response.Write(""</tr>"" & vbcrlf)");
}
```

Textarea

```
foreach(System.Data.DataRow row in dv.Table.Rows)
{
    txtstream.WriteLine("Response.Write(""<tr>"" & vbcrlf)");
    foreach(System.Data.DataColumn col in dv.Table.Columns)
    {
        txtstream.WriteLine("Response.Write(""<td  align='left'
nowrap='true'><textarea>" + row[col.Caption].ToString() + "</textarea></td>"" &
vbcrlf)");
    }
    txtstream.WriteLine("Response.Write(""</tr>"" & vbcrlf)");
}
```
Textbox

```
foreach(System.Data.DataRow row in dv.Table.Rows)
{
    txtstream.WriteLine("Response.Write(""<tr>"" & vbcrlf)");
    foreach(System.Data.DataColumn col in dv.Table.Columns)
    {
        txtstream.WriteLine("Response.Write(""<td  align='left'
nowrap='true'><input type=text value=""""" + row[col.Caption].ToString() +
"""""></input></td>"" & vbcrlf)");
    }
    txtstream.WriteLine("Response.Write(""</tr>"" & vbcrlf)");
}
```

End Code

```
txtstream.WriteLine("%>");
txtstream.WriteLine("</table>");
txtstream.WriteLine("</body>");
txtstream.WriteLine("</html>");
txtstream.Close();
```

VERTICAL

```
string cnstr = "Driver={Microsoft Access Driver (*.mdb)};DBQ=C:\NWIND.MDB";
string strQuery = "Select * From [Products]";

System.Data.ODBC.ODBCConnection cn = new
System.Data.ODBC.ODBCConnection(cnstr);
  cn.Open();

System.Data.ODBC.ODBCCommand cmd = new
System.Data.ODBC.ODBCCommand();
  cmd.Connection = cn;
  cmd.CommandType = 1;
  cmd.CommandText = strQuery;
  cmd.ExecuteNonquery();

System.Data.ODBC.ODBCDataAdapter da = new
System.Data.ODBC.ODBCDataAdapter(cmd);

System.Data.DataTable dt  as new System.Data.DataTable();
da.Fill(dt);
System.Data.DataView dv = dv.Table.DefaultView;
Scripting.FileSystemObject fso = new Scripting.FileSystemObject();
Scripting.TextStream txtstream = fso.OpenTextFile(Application.StartupPath +
"\\Products.asp",IOMode.ForWriting, True, Tristate.TristateUseDefault);
txtstream.WriteLine("<html>");
txtstream.WriteLine("<head>");
txtstream.WriteLine("<title>Products</title>");
txtstream.WriteLine("<body>");
txtstream.WriteLine("<center>");
txtstream.WriteLine("</br>");
txtstream.WriteLine("</br>");
```

For Reports:

```
txtstream.WriteLine("<table border=0 cellspacing=3 cellpadding=3>");
```

For Tables:

```
txtstream.WriteLine("<table border=1 cellspacing=3 cellpadding=3>");

txtstream.WriteLine("<%");
foreach(System.Data.DataColumn col in dv.Table.Columns)
{
    txtstream.WriteLine("Response.Write(""<tr><th align='left'
nowrap='nowrap'>" + col.Caption + "</th>""" & vbcrlf)");
```

```
foreach(System.Data.DataRow row in dv.Table.Rows)
{
    txtstream.WriteLine("Response.Write(""<td align='left' nowrap='nowrap'>"
+ row[col.Caption].ToString() + "</td>""" & vbcrlf)");
}
```

Additional Tags:

None

```
foreach(System.Data.DataRow row in dv.Table.Rows)
{
    txtstream.WriteLine("Response.Write(""<td align='left' nowrap='nowrap'>"
+ row[col.Caption].ToString() + "</td>""" & vbcrlf)");
}
```

Button

```
foreach(System.Data.DataRow row in dv.Table.Rows)
{
    txtstream.WriteLine("Response.Write(""<td align='left'
nowrap='true'><button style='width:100%;' value ='" + row[col.Caption].ToString()
+ "'>" + row[col.Caption].ToString() + "</button></td>""" & vbcrlf)");
}
```

Combobox

```
foreach(System.Data.DataRow row in dv.Table.Rows)
{
    txtstream.WriteLine("Response.Write(""<td align='left'
nowrap='true'><select><option value = """ + row[col.Caption].ToString() + """>" +
row[col.Caption].ToString() + "</option></select></td>""" & vbcrlf)");
}
```

Div

```
foreach(System.Data.DataRow row in dv.Table.Rows)
{
    txtstream.WriteLine("Response.Write(""<td align='left'
nowrap='true'><div>" + row[col.Caption].ToString() + "</div></td>""" & vbcrlf)");
}
```

Link

```
foreach(System.Data.DataRow row in dv.Table.Rows)
{
    txtstream.WriteLine("Response.Write(""<td align='left' nowrap='true'><a
href='" + row[col.Caption].ToString() + "'>" + row[col.Caption].ToString() +
"</a></td>"" & vbcrlf)");
}
```

Listbox

```
foreach(System.Data.DataRow row in dv.Table.Rows)
{
    txtstream.WriteLine("Response.Write(""<td  align='left'
nowrap='true'><select multiple><option value = """ + row[col.Caption].ToString() +
"""">" + row[col.Caption].ToString() + "</option></select></td>"" & vbcrlf)");
}
```

Span

```
foreach(System.Data.DataRow row in dv.Table.Rows)
{
    txtstream.WriteLine("Response.Write(""<td  align='left'
nowrap='true'><span>" + row[col.Caption].ToString() + "</span></td>"" &
vbcrlf)");
}
```

Textarea

```
foreach(System.Data.DataRow row in dv.Table.Rows)
{
    txtstream.WriteLine("Response.Write(""<td  align='left'
nowrap='true'><textarea>" + row[col.Caption].ToString() + "</textarea></td>"" &
vbcrlf)");
}
```

Textbox

```
foreach(System.Data.DataRow row in dv.Table.Rows)
{
    txtstream.WriteLine("Response.Write(""<td  align='left'
nowrap='true'><input type=text value=""" + row[col.Caption].ToString() +
"""></input></td>"" & vbcrlf)");
}
```

```
    txtstream.WriteLine("Response.Write("""</tr>""" & vbcrlf)");
}
txtstream.WriteLine("%>");
txtstream.WriteLine("</table>");
txtstream.WriteLine("</body>");
txtstream.WriteLine("</html>");
txtstream.Close();
```

ASPX EXAMPLES

Yes you can!

B elow, are examples of using ODBC, the DataTable and ASP. And just in case you are wondering, I use none as meaning no additional tags between the <td></td>

HORIZONTAL

```
Scripting.FileSystemObject fso = new Scripting.FileSystemObject();
Scripting.TextStream txtstream = fso.OpenTextFile(Application.StartupPath +
"\\Products.asp",IOMode.ForWriting, True, Tristate.TristateUseDefault);
txtstream.WriteLine("<html>");
txtstream.WriteLine("<head>");
txtstream.WriteLine("<title>Products</title>");
txtstream.WriteLine("<body>");
```

For Reports:

```
txtstream.WriteLine("<table border=0 cellspacing=3 cellpadding=3>");
```

For Tables:

```
txtstream.WriteLine("<table border=1 cellspacing=3 cellpadding=3>");

txtstream.WriteLine("<%");
```

```
    txtstream.WriteLine("Response.Write(""<tr>"" & vbcrlf)");
    foreach(System.Data.DataColumn col in dv.Table.Columns)
    {
        txtstream.WriteLine("Response.Write(""<th align='left' nowrap='nowrap'>" +
col.Caption + "</th>"" & vbcrlf)");
    }
    txtstream.WriteLine("Response.Write(""</tr>"" & vbcrlf)");
```

Additional Tags:

None

```
    foreach(System.Data.DataRow row in dv.Table.Rows)
    {
        txtstream.WriteLine("Response.Write(""<tr>"" & vbcrlf)");
        foreach(System.Data.DataColumn col in dv.Table.Columns)
        {
            txtstream.WriteLine("Response.Write(""<td  align='left' nowrap='nowrap'>"
+ row[col.Caption].ToString() + "</td>"" & vbcrlf)");
        }
        txtstream.WriteLine("Response.Write(""</tr>"" & vbcrlf)");
    }
```

Button

```
    foreach(System.Data.DataRow row in dv.Table.Rows)
    {
        txtstream.WriteLine("Response.Write(""<tr>"" & vbcrlf)");
        foreach(System.Data.DataColumn col in dv.Table.Columns)
        {
            txtstream.WriteLine("Response.Write(""<td  align='left'
nowrap='true'><button style='width:100%;' value ='" + row[col.Caption].ToString()
+ "'>" + row[col.Caption].ToString() + "</button></td>"" & vbcrlf)");
        }
        txtstream.WriteLine("Response.Write(""</tr>"" & vbcrlf)");
    }
```

Combobox

```
    foreach(System.Data.DataRow row in dv.Table.Rows)
    {
        txtstream.WriteLine("Response.Write(""<tr>"" & vbcrlf)");
        foreach(System.Data.DataColumn col in dv.Table.Columns)
        {
            txtstream.WriteLine("Response.Write(""<td  align='left'
nowrap='true'><select><option value = """" + row[col.Caption].ToString() + """">" +
row[col.Caption].ToString() + "</option></select></td>"" & vbcrlf)");
```

```
        }
        txtstream.WriteLine("Response.Write(""</tr>"" & vbcrlf)");
    }
```

Div

```
    foreach(System.Data.DataRow row in dv.Table.Rows)
    {
        txtstream.WriteLine("Response.Write(""<tr>"" & vbcrlf)");
        foreach(System.Data.DataColumn col in dv.Table.Columns)
        {
            txtstream.WriteLine("Response.Write(""<td  align='left'
nowrap='true'><div>" + row[col.Caption].ToString() + "</div></td>"" & vbcrlf)");
        }
        txtstream.WriteLine("Response.Write(""</tr>"" & vbcrlf)");
    }
```

Link

```
    foreach(System.Data.DataRow row in dv.Table.Rows)
    {
        txtstream.WriteLine("Response.Write(""<tr>"" & vbcrlf)");
        foreach(System.Data.DataColumn col in dv.Table.Columns)
        {
            txtstream.WriteLine("Response.Write(""<td  align='left' nowrap='true'><a
href='" + row[col.Caption].ToString() + "'>" + row[col.Caption].ToString() +
"</a></td>"" & vbcrlf)");
        }
        txtstream.WriteLine("Response.Write(""</tr>"" & vbcrlf)");
    }
```

Listbox

```
    foreach(System.Data.DataRow row in dv.Table.Rows)
    {
        txtstream.WriteLine("Response.Write(""<tr>"" & vbcrlf)");
        foreach(System.Data.DataColumn col in dv.Table.Columns)
        {
            txtstream.WriteLine("Response.Write(""<td  align='left'
nowrap='true'><select multiple><option value = """ + row[col.Caption].ToString() +
"""">" + row[col.Caption].ToString() + "</option></select></td>"" & vbcrlf)");
        }
        txtstream.WriteLine("Response.Write(""</tr>"" & vbcrlf)");
    }
```

```
foreach(System.Data.DataRow row in dv.Table.Rows)
{
    txtstream.WriteLine("Response.Write(""<tr>"" & vbcrlf)");
    foreach(System.Data.DataColumn col in dv.Table.Columns)
    {
        txtstream.WriteLine("Response.Write(""<td align='left'
nowrap='true'><span>" + row[col.Caption].ToString() + "</span></td>"" &
vbcrlf)");
    }
    txtstream.WriteLine("Response.Write(""</tr>"" & vbcrlf)");
}
```

```
foreach(System.Data.DataRow row in dv.Table.Rows)
{
    txtstream.WriteLine("Response.Write(""<tr>"" & vbcrlf)");
    foreach(System.Data.DataColumn col in dv.Table.Columns)
    {
        txtstream.WriteLine("Response.Write(""<td align='left'
nowrap='true'><textarea>" + row[col.Caption].ToString() + "</textarea></td>"" &
vbcrlf)");
    }
    txtstream.WriteLine("Response.Write(""</tr>"" & vbcrlf)");
}
```

```
foreach(System.Data.DataRow row in dv.Table.Rows)
{
    txtstream.WriteLine("Response.Write(""<tr>"" & vbcrlf)");
    foreach(System.Data.DataColumn col in dv.Table.Columns)
    {
        txtstream.WriteLine("Response.Write(""<td align='left'
nowrap='true'><input type=text value=""" + row[col.Caption].ToString() +
"""></input></td>"" & vbcrlf)");
    }
    txtstream.WriteLine("Response.Write(""</tr>"" & vbcrlf)");
}
```

```
txtstream.WriteLine("%>");
txtstream.WriteLine("</table>");
txtstream.WriteLine("</body>");
txtstream.WriteLine("</html>");
```

```
txtstream.Close();
```

VERTICAL

```
Scripting.FileSystemObject fso = new Scripting.FileSystemObject();
Scripting.TextStream txtstream = fso.OpenTextFile(Application.StartupPath +
"\\Products.asp",IOMode.ForWriting, True, Tristate.TristateUseDefault);
txtstream.WriteLine("<html>");
txtstream.WriteLine("<head>");
txtstream.WriteLine("<title>Products</title>");
txtstream.WriteLine("<body>");
txtstream.WriteLine("<center>");
txtstream.WriteLine("</br>");
txtstream.WriteLine("</br>");
```

For Reports:

```
txtstream.WriteLine("<table border=0 cellspacing=3 cellpadding=3>");
```

For Tables:

```
txtstream.WriteLine("<table border=1 cellspacing=3 cellpadding=3>");

txtstream.WriteLine("<%");
foreach(System.Data.DataColumn col in dv.Table.Columns)
{
    txtstream.WriteLine("Response.Write(""<tr><th align='left'
nowrap='nowrap'>" + col.Caption + "</th>""" & vbcrlf)");
```

None

```
foreach(System.Data.DataRow row in dv.Table.Rows)
{
    txtstream.WriteLine("Response.Write(""<td  align='left' nowrap='nowrap'>"
+ row[col.Caption].ToString() + "</td>""" & vbcrlf)");
}
```

Additional Tags:

```
    foreach(System.Data.DataRow row in dv.Table.Rows)
    {
       txtstream.WriteLine("Response.Write(""<td align='left' nowrap='nowrap'>"
+ row[col.Caption].ToString() + "</td>""" & vbcrlf)");
    }
```

```
    foreach(System.Data.DataRow row in dv.Table.Rows)
    {
       txtstream.WriteLine("Response.Write(""<td align='left'
nowrap='true'><button style='width:100%;' value ='" + row[col.Caption].ToString()
+ "'>" + row[col.Caption].ToString() + "</button></td>""" & vbcrlf)");
    }
```

```
    foreach(System.Data.DataRow row in dv.Table.Rows)
    {
       txtstream.WriteLine("Response.Write(""<td align='left'
nowrap='true'><select><option value = """ + row[col.Caption].ToString() + """">" +
row[col.Caption].ToString() + "</option></select></td>""" & vbcrlf)");
    }
```

```
    foreach(System.Data.DataRow row in dv.Table.Rows)
    {
       txtstream.WriteLine("Response.Write(""<td align='left'
nowrap='true'><div>" + row[col.Caption].ToString() + "</div></td>""" & vbcrlf)");
    }
```

```
    foreach(System.Data.DataRow row in dv.Table.Rows)
    {
       txtstream.WriteLine("Response.Write(""<td align='left' nowrap='true'><a
href='" + row[col.Caption].ToString() + "'>" + row[col.Caption].ToString() +
"</a></td>""" & vbcrlf)");
    }
```

```
    foreach(System.Data.DataRow row in dv.Table.Rows)
    {
        txtstream.WriteLine("Response.Write(""<td  align='left'
nowrap='true'><select multiple><option value = """" + row[col.Caption].ToString() +
"""">" + row[col.Caption].ToString() + "</option></select></td>"" & vbcrlf)");
    }
```

Span

```
    foreach(System.Data.DataRow row in dv.Table.Rows)
    {
        txtstream.WriteLine("Response.Write(""<td  align='left'
nowrap='true'><span>" + row[col.Caption].ToString() + "</span></td>"" &
vbcrlf)");
    }
```

Textarea

```
    foreach(System.Data.DataRow row in dv.Table.Rows)
    {
        txtstream.WriteLine("Response.Write(""<td  align='left'
nowrap='true'><textarea>" + row[col.Caption].ToString() + "</textarea></td>"" &
vbcrlf)");
    }
```

Textbox

```
    foreach(System.Data.DataRow row in dv.Table.Rows)
    {
        txtstream.WriteLine("Response.Write(""<td  align='left'
nowrap='true'><input type=text value="""" + row[col.Caption].ToString() +
""""></input></td>"" & vbcrlf)");
    }
```

End Code

```
        txtstream.WriteLine("Response.Write(""</tr>"" & vbcrlf)");
    }
    txtstream.WriteLine("%>");
    txtstream.WriteLine("</table>");
    txtstream.WriteLine("</body>");
    txtstream.WriteLine("</html>");
    txtstream.Close();
```

HTA EXAMPLES

Let's do it!

Below, are examples of using ODBC, the DataTable and ASP. And just in case you are wondering, I use none as meaning no additional tags between the <td></td>

HORIZONTAL

```
Scripting.FileSystemObject fso = new Scripting.FileSystemObject();
Scripting.TextStream txtstream = fso.OpenTextFile(Application.StartupPath +
"\\Products.asp",IOMode.ForWriting, True, Tristate.TristateUseDefault);
txtstream.WriteLine("<html>");
txtstream.WriteLine("<head>");
txtstream.WriteLine("<HTA:APPLICATION ");
txtstream.WriteLine("ID = 'Products' ");
txtstream.WriteLine("APPLICATIONNAME = 'Products' ");
txtstream.WriteLine("SCROLL = 'yes' ");
txtstream.WriteLine("SINGLEINSTANCE = 'yes' ");
txtstream.WriteLine("WINDOWSTATE = 'maximize' >");
txtstream.WriteLine("<title>Products</title>");
txtstream.WriteLine("<body>");
```

For Reports:

```
txtstream.WriteLine("<table border=0 cellspacing=3 cellpadding=3>");
```

For Tables:

```
txtstream.WriteLine("<table border=1 cellspacing=3 cellpadding=3>");

txtstream.WriteLine("<%");
txtstream.WriteLine("<tr>");
foreach(System.Data.DataColumn col in dv.Table.Columns)
{
    txtstream.WriteLine("<th align='left' nowrap='nowrap'>" +   col.Caption +
"</th>");
}
txtstream.WriteLine("</tr>");
```

Additional Tags:

None

```
foreach(System.Data.DataRow row in dv.Table.Rows)
{
    txtstream.WriteLine("<tr>");
    foreach(System.Data.DataColumn col in dv.Table.Columns)
    {
        txtstream.WriteLine("<td align='left' nowrap='nowrap'>" +
row[col.Caption].ToString() + "</td>");
    }
    txtstream.WriteLine("</tr>");
}
```

Button

```
foreach(System.Data.DataRow row in dv.Table.Rows)
{
    txtstream.WriteLine("<tr>");
    foreach(System.Data.DataColumn col in dv.Table.Columns)
    {
        txtstream.WriteLine("<td  align='left' nowrap='true'><button
style='width:100%;' value ='" + row[col.Caption].ToString() + "'>" +
row[col.Caption].ToString() + "</button></td>");
    }
    txtstream.WriteLine("</tr>");
}
```

Combobox

```
foreach(System.Data.DataRow row in dv.Table.Rows)
{
```

```
        txtstream.WriteLine("<tr>");
        foreach(System.Data.DataColumn col in dv.Table.Columns)
        {
            txtstream.WriteLine("<td  align='left' nowrap='true'><select><option value
= """" + row[col.Caption].ToString() + """">" + row[col.Caption].ToString() +
"</option></select></td>");
        }
        txtstream.WriteLine("</tr>");
    }
```

Div

```
    foreach(System.Data.DataRow row in dv.Table.Rows)
    {
        txtstream.WriteLine("<tr>");
        foreach(System.Data.DataColumn col in dv.Table.Columns)
        {
            txtstream.WriteLine("<td  align='left' nowrap='true'><div>" +
row[col.Caption].ToString() + "</div></td>");
        }
        txtstream.WriteLine("</tr>");
    }
```

Link

```
    foreach(System.Data.DataRow row in dv.Table.Rows)
    {
        txtstream.WriteLine("<tr>");
        foreach(System.Data.DataColumn col in dv.Table.Columns)
        {
            txtstream.WriteLine("<td  align='left' nowrap='true'><a href='" +
row[col.Caption].ToString() + "'>" + row[col.Caption].ToString() + "</a></td>");
        }
        txtstream.WriteLine("</tr>");
    }
```

Listbox

```
    foreach(System.Data.DataRow row in dv.Table.Rows)
    {
        txtstream.WriteLine("<tr>");
        foreach(System.Data.DataColumn col in dv.Table.Columns)
        {
            txtstream.WriteLine("<td  align='left' nowrap='true'><select
multiple><option value = """" + row[col.Caption].ToString() + """">" +
row[col.Caption].ToString() + "</option></select></td>");
        }
```

```
    txtstream.WriteLine("</tr>");
  }
```

Span

```
  foreach(System.Data.DataRow row in dv.Table.Rows)
  {
    txtstream.WriteLine("<tr>");
    foreach(System.Data.DataColumn col in dv.Table.Columns)
    {
      txtstream.WriteLine("<td align='left' nowrap='true'><span>" +
row[col.Caption].ToString() + "</span></td>");
    }
    txtstream.WriteLine("</tr>");
  }
```

Textarea

```
  foreach(System.Data.DataRow row in dv.Table.Rows)
  {
    txtstream.WriteLine("<tr>");
    foreach(System.Data.DataColumn col in dv.Table.Columns)
    {
      txtstream.WriteLine("<td align='left' nowrap='true'><textarea>" +
row[col.Caption].ToString() + "</textarea></td>");
    }
    txtstream.WriteLine("</tr>");
  }
```
Textbox

```
  foreach(System.Data.DataRow row in dv.Table.Rows)
  {
    txtstream.WriteLine("<tr>");
    foreach(System.Data.DataColumn col in dv.Table.Columns)
    {
      txtstream.WriteLine("<td align='left' nowrap='true'><input type=text
value='''" + row[col.Caption].ToString() + "'''></input></td>");
    }
    txtstream.WriteLine("</tr>");
  }
```

End Code

```
  txtstream.WriteLine("%>");
  txtstream.WriteLine("</table>");
  txtstream.WriteLine("</body>");
```

```
txtstream.WriteLine("</html>");
txtstream.Close();
```

VERTICAL

```
string cnstr = "Driver={Microsoft Access Driver (*.mdb)};DBQ=C:\NWIND.MDB";
string strQuery = "Select * From [Products]";

System.Data.ODBC.ODBCConnection cn = new
System.Data.ODBC.ODBCConnection(cnstr);
cn.Open();

System.Data.ODBC.ODBCCommand cmd = new
System.Data.ODBC.ODBCCommand();
cmd.Connection = cn;
cmd.CommandType = 1;
cmd.CommandText = strQuery;
cmd.ExecuteNonquery();

System.Data.ODBC.ODBCDataAdapter da = new
System.Data.ODBC.ODBCDataAdapter(cmd);

System.Data.DataTable dt  as new System.Data.DataTable();
da.Fill(dt);
System.Data.DataView dv = dv.Table.DefaultView;
Scripting.FileSystemObject fso = new Scripting.FileSystemObject();
Scripting.TextStream txtstream = fso.OpenTextFile(Application.StartupPath +
"\\Products.asp",IOMode.ForWriting, True, Tristate.TristateUseDefault);
txtstream.WriteLine("<html>");
txtstream.WriteLine("<head>");
txtstream.WriteLine("<title>Products</title>");
txtstream.WriteLine("<body>");
txtstream.WriteLine("<center>");
txtstream.WriteLine("</br>");
txtstream.WriteLine("</br>");
```

For Reports:

```
txtstream.WriteLine("<table border=0 cellspacing=3 cellpadding=3>");
```

For Tables:

```
txtstream.WriteLine("<table border=1 cellspacing=3 cellpadding=3>");

txtstream.WriteLine("<%");
foreach(System.Data.DataColumn col in dv.Table.Columns)
```

```
    {
        txtstream.WriteLine("<tr><th align='left' nowrap='nowrap'>" + col.Caption +
"</th>");
```

```
        foreach(System.Data.DataRow row in dv.Table.Rows)
        {
            txtstream.WriteLine("<td align='left' nowrap='nowrap'>" +
row[col.Caption].ToString() + "</td>");
        }
```

Additional Tags:

None

```
        foreach(System.Data.DataRow row in dv.Table.Rows)
        {
            txtstream.WriteLine("<td  align='left' nowrap='nowrap'>" +
row[col.Caption].ToString() + "</td>");
        }
```

Button

```
        foreach(System.Data.DataRow row in dv.Table.Rows)
        {
            txtstream.WriteLine("<td  align='left' nowrap='true'><button
style='width:100%;' value ='" + row[col.Caption].ToString() + "'>" +
row[col.Caption].ToString() + "</button></td>");
        }
```

Combobox

```
        foreach(System.Data.DataRow row in dv.Table.Rows)
        {
            txtstream.WriteLine("<td  align='left' nowrap='true'><select><option value
= "'" + row[col.Caption].ToString() + "'">" + row[col.Caption].ToString() +
"</option></select></td>");
        }
```

Div

```
    foreach(System.Data.DataRow row in dv.Table.Rows)
    {
        txtstream.WriteLine("<td align='left' nowrap='true'><div>" +
row[col.Caption].ToString() + "</div></td>");
    }
```

Link

```
    foreach(System.Data.DataRow row in dv.Table.Rows)
    {
        txtstream.WriteLine("<td align='left' nowrap='true'><a href='" +
row[col.Caption].ToString() + "'>" + row[col.Caption].ToString() + "</a></td>");
    }
```

Listbox

```
    foreach(System.Data.DataRow row in dv.Table.Rows)
    {
        txtstream.WriteLine("<td align='left' nowrap='true'><select
multiple><option value = "'" + row[col.Caption].ToString() + "'">" +
row[col.Caption].ToString() + "</option></select></td>");
    }
```

Span

```
    foreach(System.Data.DataRow row in dv.Table.Rows)
    {
        txtstream.WriteLine("<td align='left' nowrap='true'><span>" +
row[col.Caption].ToString() + "</span></td>");
    }
```

Textarea

```
    foreach(System.Data.DataRow row in dv.Table.Rows)
    {
        txtstream.WriteLine("<td align='left' nowrap='true'><textarea>" +
row[col.Caption].ToString() + "</textarea></td>");
    }
```

Textbox

```
    foreach(System.Data.DataRow row in dv.Table.Rows)
    {
        txtstream.WriteLine("<td align='left' nowrap='true'><input type=text
value="'" + row[col.Caption].ToString() + "'"></input></td>");
    }
```

```
    txtstream.WriteLine("</tr>");
}
txtstream.WriteLine("%>");
txtstream.WriteLine("</table>");
txtstream.WriteLine("</body>");
txtstream.WriteLine("</html>");
txtstream.Close();
```

HTA EXAMPLES

Let's do it!

B
elow, are examples of using ODBC, the DataTable and ASP. And just in case you are wondering, I use none as meaning no additional tags between the <td></td>

HORIZONTAL

```
Scripting.FileSystemObject fso = new Scripting.FileSystemObject();
Scripting.TextStream txtstream = fso.OpenTextFile(Application.StartupPath +
"\\Products.asp",IOMode.ForWriting, True, Tristate.TristateUseDefault);
txtstream.WriteLine("<html>");
txtstream.WriteLine("<head>");
txtstream.WriteLine("<title>Products</title>");
txtstream.WriteLine("<body>");
```

For Reports:

```
txtstream.WriteLine("<table border=0 cellspacing=3 cellpadding=3>");
```

For Tables:

```
txtstream.WriteLine("<table border=1 cellspacing=3 cellpadding=3>");
```

```
txtstream.WriteLine("<%");
txtstream.WriteLine("<tr>");
foreach(System.Data.DataColumn col in dv.Table.Columns)
{
    txtstream.WriteLine("<th align='left' nowrap='nowrap'>" +    col.Caption +
"</th>");
}
txtstream.WriteLine("</tr>");
```

Additional Tags:

None

```
foreach(System.Data.DataRow row in dv.Table.Rows)
{
    txtstream.WriteLine("<tr>");
    foreach(System.Data.DataColumn col in dv.Table.Columns)
    {
        txtstream.WriteLine("<td  align='left' nowrap='nowrap'>" +
row[col.Caption].ToString() + "</td>");
    }
    txtstream.WriteLine("</tr>");
}
```

Button

```
foreach(System.Data.DataRow row in dv.Table.Rows)
{
    txtstream.WriteLine("<tr>");
    foreach(System.Data.DataColumn col in dv.Table.Columns)
    {
        txtstream.WriteLine("<td  align='left' nowrap='true'><button
style='width:100%;' value ='" + row[col.Caption].ToString() + "'>" +
row[col.Caption].ToString() + "</button></td>");
    }
    txtstream.WriteLine("</tr>");
}
```

Combobox

```
foreach(System.Data.DataRow row in dv.Table.Rows)
{
    txtstream.WriteLine("<tr>");
    foreach(System.Data.DataColumn col in dv.Table.Columns)
    {
```

```
      txtstream.WriteLine("<td  align='left' nowrap='true'><select><option value
= "'" + row[col.Caption].ToString() + "'">" + row[col.Caption].ToString() +
"</option></select></td>");
      }
    txtstream.WriteLine("</tr>");
  }
```

Div

```
  foreach(System.Data.DataRow row in dv.Table.Rows)
  {
    txtstream.WriteLine("<tr>");
    foreach(System.Data.DataColumn col in dv.Table.Columns)
    {
      txtstream.WriteLine("<td  align='left' nowrap='true'><div>" +
row[col.Caption].ToString() + "</div></td>");
    }
    txtstream.WriteLine("</tr>");
  }
```

Link

```
  foreach(System.Data.DataRow row in dv.Table.Rows)
  {
    txtstream.WriteLine("<tr>");
    foreach(System.Data.DataColumn col in dv.Table.Columns)
    {
      txtstream.WriteLine("<td  align='left' nowrap='true'><a href='" +
row[col.Caption].ToString() + "'>" + row[col.Caption].ToString() + "</a></td>");
    }
    txtstream.WriteLine("</tr>");
  }
```

Listbox

```
  foreach(System.Data.DataRow row in dv.Table.Rows)
  {
    txtstream.WriteLine("<tr>");
    foreach(System.Data.DataColumn col in dv.Table.Columns)
    {
      txtstream.WriteLine("<td  align='left' nowrap='true'><select
multiple><option value = "'" + row[col.Caption].ToString() + "'">" +
row[col.Caption].ToString() + "</option></select></td>");
    }
    txtstream.WriteLine("</tr>");
  }
```

```
foreach(System.Data.DataRow row in dv.Table.Rows)
{
    txtstream.WriteLine("<tr>");
    foreach(System.Data.DataColumn col in dv.Table.Columns)
    {
        txtstream.WriteLine("<td align='left' nowrap='true'><span>" +
row[col.Caption].ToString() + "</span></td>");
    }
    txtstream.WriteLine("</tr>");
}
```

Textarea

```
foreach(System.Data.DataRow row in dv.Table.Rows)
{
    txtstream.WriteLine("<tr>");
    foreach(System.Data.DataColumn col in dv.Table.Columns)
    {
        txtstream.WriteLine("<td align='left' nowrap='true'><textarea>" +
row[col.Caption].ToString() + "</textarea></td>");
    }
    txtstream.WriteLine("</tr>");
}
```

Textbox

```
foreach(System.Data.DataRow row in dv.Table.Rows)
{
    txtstream.WriteLine("<tr>");
    foreach(System.Data.DataColumn col in dv.Table.Columns)
    {
        txtstream.WriteLine("<td align='left' nowrap='true'><input type=text
value=""" + row[col.Caption].ToString() + """></input></td>");
    }
    txtstream.WriteLine("</tr>");
}
```

End Code

```
txtstream.WriteLine("%>");
txtstream.WriteLine("</table>");
txtstream.WriteLine("</body>");
txtstream.WriteLine("</html>");
txtstream.Close();
```

VERTICAL

```
string cnstr = "Driver={Microsoft Access Driver (*.mdb)};DBQ=C:\NWIND.MDB";
string strQuery = "Select * From [Products]";

System.Data.ODBC.ODBCConnection cn = new
System.Data.ODBC.ODBCConnection(cnstr);
  cn.Open();

System.Data.ODBC.ODBCCommand cmd = new
System.Data.ODBC.ODBCCommand();
  cmd.Connection = cn;
  cmd.CommandType = 1;
  cmd.CommandText = strQuery;
  cmd.ExecuteNonquery();

System.Data.ODBC.ODBCDataAdapter da = new
System.Data.ODBC.ODBCDataAdapter(cmd);

System.Data.DataTable dt  as new System.Data.DataTable();
  da.Fill(dt);
System.Data.DataView dv = dv.Table.DefaultView;
Scripting.FileSystemObject fso = new Scripting.FileSystemObject();
Scripting.TextStream txtstream = fso.OpenTextFile(Application.StartupPath +
"\\Products.asp",IOMode.ForWriting, True, Tristate.TristateUseDefault);
  txtstream.WriteLine("<html>");
  txtstream.WriteLine("<head>");
  txtstream.WriteLine("<title>Products</title>");
  txtstream.WriteLine("<body>");
  txtstream.WriteLine("<center>");
  txtstream.WriteLine("</br>");
  txtstream.WriteLine("</br>");
```

For Reports:

```
  txtstream.WriteLine("<table border=0 cellspacing=3 cellpadding=3>");
```

For Tables:

```
  txtstream.WriteLine("<table border=1 cellspacing=3 cellpadding=3>");

  txtstream.WriteLine("<%");
  foreach(System.Data.DataColumn col in dv.Table.Columns)
  {
    txtstream.WriteLine("<tr><th align='left' nowrap='nowrap'>" + col.Caption +
"</th>");
```

```
foreach(System.Data.DataRow row in dv.Table.Rows)
{
    txtstream.WriteLine("<td align='left' nowrap='nowrap'>" +
row[col.Caption].ToString() + "</td>");
}
```

Additional Tags:

None

```
foreach(System.Data.DataRow row in dv.Table.Rows)
{
    txtstream.WriteLine("<td align='left' nowrap='nowrap'>" +
row[col.Caption].ToString() + "</td>");
}
```

Button

```
foreach(System.Data.DataRow row in dv.Table.Rows)
{
    txtstream.WriteLine("<td align='left' nowrap='true'><button
style='width:100%;' value ='" + row[col.Caption].ToString() + "'>" +
row[col.Caption].ToString() + "</button></td>");
}
```

Combobox

```
foreach(System.Data.DataRow row in dv.Table.Rows)
{
    txtstream.WriteLine("<td align='left' nowrap='true'><select><option value
= '''" + row[col.Caption].ToString() + "'''>" + row[col.Caption].ToString() +
"</option></select></td>");
}
```

Div

```
foreach(System.Data.DataRow row in dv.Table.Rows)
{
```

```
    txtstream.WriteLine("<td align='left' nowrap='true'><div>" +
row[col.Caption].ToString() + "</div></td>");
    }
```

Link

```
    foreach(System.Data.DataRow row in dv.Table.Rows)
    {
        txtstream.WriteLine("<td align='left' nowrap='true'><a href='" +
row[col.Caption].ToString() + "'>" + row[col.Caption].ToString() + "</a></td>");
    }
```

Listbox

```
    foreach(System.Data.DataRow row in dv.Table.Rows)
    {
        txtstream.WriteLine("<td align='left' nowrap='true'><select
multiple><option value = """ + row[col.Caption].ToString() + """>" +
row[col.Caption].ToString() + "</option></select></td>");
    }
```

Span

```
    foreach(System.Data.DataRow row in dv.Table.Rows)
    {
        txtstream.WriteLine("<td align='left' nowrap='true'><span>" +
row[col.Caption].ToString() + "</span></td>");
    }
```

Textarea

```
    foreach(System.Data.DataRow row in dv.Table.Rows)
    {
        txtstream.WriteLine("<td align='left' nowrap='true'><textarea>" +
row[col.Caption].ToString() + "</textarea></td>");
    }
```

Textbox

```
    foreach(System.Data.DataRow row in dv.Table.Rows)
    {
        txtstream.WriteLine("<td align='left' nowrap='true'><input type=text
value=""" + row[col.Caption].ToString() + """></input></td>");
    }
```

```
    txtstream.WriteLine("</tr>");
}
txtstream.WriteLine("%>");
txtstream.WriteLine("</table>");
txtstream.WriteLine("</body>");
txtstream.WriteLine("</html>");
txtstream.Close();
```

DELIMITED TEXT FILES

B ELOW ARE THE POPULAR EXAMPLES OF DIFFERENT DELIMITED TEXT
FILES.

COLON DELIMITED HORIZONTAL VIEW

```
String tempstr = "";

Scripting.FileSystemObject fso = new Scripting.FileSystemObject();
Scripting.TextStream txtstream = fso.OpenTextFile(Application.StartupPath +
"\Products.txt",IOMode.ForWriting, True, Tristate.TristateUseDefault);
foreach(System.Data.DataColumn col in dv.Table.Columns)
{
   if (tempstr != "")
   {
      tempstr = tempstr + ":";
   }
   tempstr = tempstr + col.Caption;
}
txtstream.WriteLine(tempstr);
tempstr = "";

foreach(System.Data.DataRow row in dv.Table.Rows)
{
   foreach(System.Data.DataColumn col in dv.Table.Columns)
   {
      if (tempstr != "")
      {
         tempstr = tempstr + ":";
```

```
      }
      tempstr = tempstr + (char)34 + row[col.Caption].ToString() + (char)34;
   }
   txtstream.WriteLine(tempstr);
   tempstr = "";

}
txtstream.Close();
```

COLON DELIMITED VERTICAL VIEW

```
String tempstr = "";


Scripting.FileSystemObject fso = new Scripting.FileSystemObject();
Scripting.TextStream txtstream = fso.OpenTextFile(Application.StartupPath +
"\Products.txt",IOMode.ForWriting, True, Tristate.TristateUseDefault);
foreach(System.Data.DataColumn col in dv.Table.Columns)
{
   tempstr = col.Caption;
   foreach(System.Data.DataRow row in dv.Table.Rows)
   {
      if (tempstr != "")
      {
         tempstr = tempstr + ":";
      }
         tempstr = tempstr + (char)34 + row[col.Caption].ToString() + (char)34;
   }
   txtstream.WriteLine(tempstr);
   tempstr = "";

}
txtstream.Close();
```

COMMA DELIMITED HORIZONTAL VIEW

```
String tempstr = "";

Scripting.FileSystemObject fso = new Scripting.FileSystemObject();
Scripting.TextStream txtstream = fso.OpenTextFile(Application.StartupPath +
"\Products.csv",IOMode.ForWriting, True, Tristate.TristateUseDefault);
foreach(System.Data.DataColumn col in dv.Table.Columns)
{
   if (tempstr != "")
   {
```

```
         tempstr = tempstr + ",";
      }
      tempstr = tempstr + col.Caption;
}
txtstream.WriteLine(tempstr);
tempstr = "";

foreach(System.Data.DataRow row in dv.Table.Rows)
{
   foreach(System.Data.DataColumn col in dv.Table.Columns)
   {
      if (tempstr != "")
      {
         tempstr = tempstr + ",";
      }
         tempstr = tempstr + (char)34 + row[col.Caption].ToString() + (char)34;
      }
      txtstream.WriteLine(tempstr);
      tempstr = "";

}
txtstream.Close();
```

COMMA DELIMITED VERTICAL VIEW

```
String tempstr = "";

Scripting.FileSystemObject fso = new Scripting.FileSystemObject();
Scripting.TextStream txtstream = fso.OpenTextFile(Application.StartupPath +
"\Products.csv",IOMode.ForWriting, True, Tristate.TristateUseDefault);
foreach(System.Data.DataColumn col in dv.Table.Columns)
{
   tempstr = col.Caption;
   foreach(System.Data.DataRow row in dv.Table.Rows)
   {
      if (tempstr != "")
      {
         tempstr = tempstr + ",";
      }
         tempstr = tempstr + (char)34 + row[col.Caption].ToString() + (char)34;
      }
   }
   txtstream.WriteLine(tempstr);
   tempstr = "";

}
txtstream.Close();
```

EXCLAMATION DELIMITED HORIZONTAL VIEW

```
String tempstr = "";

Scripting.FileSystemObject fso = new Scripting.FileSystemObject();
Scripting.TextStream txtstream = fso.OpenTextFile(Application.StartupPath +
"\Products.txt",IOMode.ForWriting, True, Tristate.TristateUseDefault);
foreach(System.Data.DataColumn col in dv.Table.Columns)
{
   if (tempstr != "")
   {
      tempstr = tempstr + "!";
   }
   tempstr = tempstr + col.Caption;
}
txtstream.WriteLine(tempstr);
tempstr = "";

foreach(System.Data.DataRow row in dv.Table.Rows)
{
   foreach(System.Data.DataColumn col in dv.Table.Columns)
   {
      if (tempstr != "")
      {
         tempstr = tempstr + "!";
      }
      tempstr = tempstr + (char)34 + row[col.Caption].ToString() + (char)34;
   }
   txtstream.WriteLine(tempstr);
   tempstr = "";

}
txtstream.Close();
```

EXCLAMATION DELIMITED VERTICAL VIEW

```
String tempstr = "";

Scripting.FileSystemObject fso = new Scripting.FileSystemObject();
Scripting.TextStream txtstream = fso.OpenTextFile(Application.StartupPath +
"\Products.txt",IOMode.ForWriting, True, Tristate.TristateUseDefault);
foreach(System.Data.DataColumn col in dv.Table.Columns)
{
```

```
   tempstr = col.Caption;
   foreach(System.Data.DataRow row in dv.Table.Rows)
   {
      if (tempstr != "")
      {
         tempstr = tempstr + "!";
      }
         tempstr = tempstr + (char)34 + row[col.Caption].ToString() + (char)34;
      }
   }
   txtstream.WriteLine(tempstr);
   tempstr = "";

}
txtstream.Close();
```

SEMI-COLON DELIMITED HORIZONTAL VIEW

```
String tempstr = "";

Scripting.FileSystemObject fso = new Scripting.FileSystemObject();
Scripting.TextStream txtstream = fso.OpenTextFile(Application.StartupPath +
"\Products.txt",IOMode.ForWriting, True, Tristate.TristateUseDefault);
foreach(System.Data.DataColumn col in dv.Table.Columns)
{
   if (tempstr != "")
   {
      tempstr = tempstr + ";";
   }
   tempstr = tempstr + col.Caption;
}
txtstream.WriteLine(tempstr);
tempstr = "";

foreach(System.Data.DataRow row in dv.Table.Rows)
{
   foreach(System.Data.DataColumn col in dv.Table.Columns)
   {
      if (tempstr != "")
      {
         tempstr = tempstr + ";";
      }
         tempstr = tempstr + (char)34 + row[col.Caption].ToString() + (char)34;
      }
      txtstream.WriteLine(tempstr);
      tempstr = "";
```

```
}
txtstream.Close();
```

SEMI-COLON DELIMITED VERTICAL VIEW

```
String tempstr = "";


Scripting.FileSystemObject fso = new Scripting.FileSystemObject();
Scripting.TextStream txtstream = fso.OpenTextFile(Application.StartupPath +
"\Products.txt",IOMode.ForWriting, True, Tristate.TristateUseDefault);
foreach(System.Data.DataColumn col in dv.Table.Columns)
{
    tempstr = col.Caption;
    foreach(System.Data.DataRow row in dv.Table.Rows)
    {
        if (tempstr != "")
        {
            tempstr = tempstr + ";";
        }
        tempstr = tempstr + (char)34 + row[col.Caption].ToString() + (char)34;
    }
    txtstream.WriteLine(tempstr);
    tempstr = "";

}
txtstream.Close();
```

TAB DELIMITED HORIZONTAL VIEW

```
String tempstr = "";


Scripting.FileSystemObject fso = new Scripting.FileSystemObject();
Scripting.TextStream txtstream = fso.OpenTextFile(Application.StartupPath +
"\Products.txt",IOMode.ForWriting, True, Tristate.TristateUseDefault);
foreach(System.Data.DataColumn col in dv.Table.Columns)
{
    if (tempstr != "")
    {
        tempstr = tempstr + "\t";
    }
    tempstr = tempstr + col.Caption;
}
txtstream.WriteLine(tempstr);
tempstr = "";
```

```
foreach(System.Data.DataRow row in dv.Table.Rows)
{
   foreach(System.Data.DataColumn col in dv.Table.Columns)
   {
      if (tempstr != "")
      {
         tempstr = tempstr + "\t";
      }
      tempstr = tempstr + (char)34 + row[col.Caption].ToString() + (char)34;
   }
   txtstream.WriteLine(tempstr);
   tempstr = "";

}
txtstream.Close();
```

TAB DELIMITED VERTICAL VIEW

```
String tempstr = "";

Scripting.FileSystemObject fso = new Scripting.FileSystemObject();
Scripting.TextStream txtstream = fso.OpenTextFile(Application.StartupPath +
"\Products.txt",IOMode.ForWriting, True, Tristate.TristateUseDefault);
foreach(System.Data.DataColumn col in dv.Table.Columns)
{
   tempstr = col.Caption;
   foreach(System.Data.DataRow row in dv.Table.Rows)
   {
      if (tempstr != "")
      {
         tempstr = tempstr + "\t";
      }
      tempstr = tempstr + (char)34 + row[col.Caption].ToString() + (char)34;
   }
   txtstream.WriteLine(tempstr);
   tempstr = "";

}
txtstream.Close();
```

TILDE DELIMITED HORIZONTAL VIEW

```
String tempstr = "";
```

```
Scripting.FileSystemObject fso = new Scripting.FileSystemObject();
Scripting.TextStream txtstream = fso.OpenTextFile(Application.StartupPath +
"\Products.txt",IOMode.ForWriting, True, Tristate.TristateUseDefault);
foreach(System.Data.DataColumn col in dv.Table.Columns)
{
    if (tempstr != "")
    {
        tempstr = tempstr + "~";
    }
    tempstr = tempstr + col.Caption;
}
txtstream.WriteLine(tempstr);
tempstr = "";

foreach(System.Data.DataRow row in dv.Table.Rows)
{
    foreach(System.Data.DataColumn col in dv.Table.Columns)
    {
        if (tempstr != "")
        {
            tempstr = tempstr + "~";
        }
        tempstr = tempstr + (char)34 + row[col.Caption].ToString() + (char)34;
    }
    txtstream.WriteLine(tempstr);
    tempstr = "";

}
txtstream.Close();
```

TILDE DELIMITED VERTICAL VIEW

```
String tempstr = "";

Scripting.FileSystemObject fso = new Scripting.FileSystemObject();
Scripting.TextStream txtstream = fso.OpenTextFile(Application.StartupPath +
"\Products.txt",IOMode.ForWriting, True, Tristate.TristateUseDefault);
foreach(System.Data.DataColumn col in dv.Table.Columns)
{
    tempstr = col.Caption;
    foreach(System.Data.DataRow row in dv.Table.Rows)
    {
        if (tempstr != "")
        {
            tempstr = tempstr + "~";
        }
        tempstr = tempstr + (char)34 + row[col.Caption].ToString() + (char)34;
    }
```

```
    }
    txtstream.WriteLine(tempstr);
    tempstr = "";

}
txtstream.Close();
```

WORKING EXCEL

The Tale of three ways you can do

it

B ELOW ARE THREE EXAMPLES ON HOW TO WORK WITH EXCEL. The first will need a reference to Microsoft.Office.Interop.Excel.

HORIZONTAL AUTOMATION

```
var oExcel = new Microsoft.Office.Interop.Excel.Application();
oExcel.Visible = true;
var wb = oExcel.Workbooks.Add();
var ws = wb.Worksheets[1];
ws.Name = "Products";

int x = 1;
int y = 2;

foreach(System.Data.DataColumn col in dv.Table.Columns)
{
    ws.Cells[1, x] = col.Caption;
    x=x+1;
}
x = 1;
foreach(System.Data.DataRow row in dv.Table.Rows)
{
    foreach(System.Data.DataColumn col in dv.Table.Columns)
    {
        ws.Cells[y, x] = col.Caption;
```

```
    x=x + 1;
  }
  x = 1;
  y = y + 1;
}
ws.Columns.HorizontalAlignment = -4131;
ws.Columns.AutoFit();
```

VERTICAL AUTOMATION

```
var oExcel = new Microsoft.Office.Interop.Excel.Application();
oExcel.Visible = true;
var wb = oExcel.Workbooks.Add();
var ws = wb.Worksheets[1];
ws.Name = "Products";

int x = 1;
int y = 2;

foreach(System.Data.DataColumn col in dv.Table.Columns)
{
   ws.Cells[x, 1] = col.Caption;
   x=x+1;
}
x = 1;
foreach(System.Data.DataRow row in dv.Table.Rows)
{
   foreach(System.Data.DataColumn col in dv.Table.Columns)
   {
      ws.Cells[x, y] = col.Caption;
      x=x + 1;
   }
   x = 1;
   y = y + 1;
}
ws.Columns.HorizontalAlignment = -4131;
ws.Columns.AutoFit();
```

SPREADSHEET

```
Scripting.FileSystemObject fso = new Scripting.FileSystemObject();
Scripting.TextStream txtstream = fso.OpenTextFile(Application.StartupPath +
"\Products.xml",IOMode.ForWriting, True, Tristate.TristateUseDefault);
txtstream.WriteLine("<?xml version=""1.0""?>");
txtstream.WriteLine("<?mso-application progid=""Excel.Sheet""?>");
txtstream.WriteLine("<Workbook xmlns=""urn:schemas-microsoft-
com:office:spreadsheet"" xmlns:o=""urn:schemas-microsoft-com:office:office""
xmlns:x=""urn:schemas-microsoft-com:office:excel"" xmlns:ss=""urn:schemas-
microsoft-com:office:spreadsheet"" xmlns:html=""http://www.w3.org/TR/REC-
html40"">");
txtstream.WriteLine("  <ExcelWorkbook xmlns=""urn:schemas-microsoft-
com:office:excel"">");
txtstream.WriteLine("       <WindowHeight>11835</WindowHeight>");
txtstream.WriteLine("       <WindowWidth>18960</WindowWidth>");
txtstream.WriteLine("       <WindowTopX>120</WindowTopX>");
txtstream.WriteLine("       <WindowTopY>135</WindowTopY>");
txtstream.WriteLine("       <ProtectStructure>False</ProtectStructure>");
txtstream.WriteLine("       <ProtectWindows>False</ProtectWindows>");
txtstream.WriteLine("  </ExcelWorkbook>");
txtstream.WriteLine("  <Styles>");
txtstream.WriteLine("           <Style ss:ID=""s62"">");
txtstream.WriteLine("             <Borders/>");
txtstream.WriteLine("             <Font ss:FontName=""Calibri""
x:Family=""Swiss"" ss:Size=""11"" ss:Color=""#000000"" ss:Bold=""1""/>")
txtstream.WriteLine("           </Style>");
txtstream.WriteLine("           <Style ss:ID=""s63"">");
txtstream.WriteLine("             <Alignment ss:Horizontal=""Left""
ss:VERTICAL=""Bottom"" ss:Indent=""2""/>");
txtstream.WriteLine("             <Font ss:FontName=""Verdana""
x:Family=""Swiss"" ss:Size=""7.7"" ss:Color=""#000000""/>")
txtstream.WriteLine("           </Style>");
txtstream.WriteLine("  </Styles>");
txtstream.WriteLine("  <Worksheet ss:Name=""Win32_NetworkAdapter"">");
txtstream.WriteLine("   <Table x:FullColumns=""1"" x:FullRows=""1""
ss:DefaultRowHeight=""24.9375"">");
txtstream.WriteLine("    <Column ss:AutoFitWidth=""1"" ss:Width=""82.5""
ss:Span=""5""/>");
txtstream.WriteLine("    <Row ss:AutoFitHeight=""0"">");
foreach(System.Data.DataColumn col in dv.Table.Columns)
{
    txtstream.WriteLine("     <Cell ss:StyleID=""s62""><Data
ss:Type=""String"">" + col.Caption + "</Data></Cell>");
}
txtstream.WriteLine("    </Row>");
foreach(System.Data.DataRow row in dv.Table.Rows)
{
    txtstream.WriteLine("    <Row ss:AutoFitHeight=""0"">");
    foreach(System.Data.DataColumn col in dv.Table.Columns)
    {
```

```
    txtstream.WriteLine("        <Cell ss:StyleID="""s63"""><Data
ss:Type="""String""">" + row[col.Caption].ToString() + "</Data></Cell>");
    }
    txtstream.WriteLine("      </Row>");
}
txtstream.WriteLine("   </Table>");
txtstream.WriteLine("  </Worksheet>");
txtstream.WriteLine("</Workbook>");
txtstream.Close();
```

HORIZONTAL CSV

```
String tempstr = "";


Scripting.FileSystemObject fso = new Scripting.FileSystemObject();
Scripting.TextStream txtstream = fso.OpenTextFile(Application.StartupPath +
"\Products.csv",IOMode.ForWriting, True, Tristate.TristateUseDefault);
foreach(System.Data.DataColumn col in dv.Table.Columns)
{
   if (tempstr != "")
   {
      tempstr = tempstr + ",";
   }
   tempstr = tempstr + col.Caption;
}
txtstream.WriteLine(tempstr);
tempstr = "";

foreach(System.Data.DataRow row in dv.Table.Rows)
{
   foreach(System.Data.DataColumn col in dv.Table.Columns)
   {
      if (tempstr != "")
      {
         tempstr = tempstr + ",";
      }
         tempstr = tempstr + (char)34 + row[col.Caption].ToString() + (char)34;
   }
   txtstream.WriteLine(tempstr);
   tempstr = "";
}
txtstream.Close();

System.Diagnostics.Process.Start(Application.StartupPath +
"\\Products.csv");
```

VERTICAL CSV

```
String tempstr = "";

Scripting.FileSystemObject fso = new Scripting.FileSystemObject();
Scripting.TextStream txtstream = fso.OpenTextFile(Application.StartupPath +
"\Products.csv",IOMode.ForWriting, True, Tristate.TristateUseDefault);
foreach(System.Data.DataColumn col in dv.Table.Columns)
{
    tempstr = col.Caption;
    foreach(System.Data.DataRow row in dv.Table.Rows)
    {
        if (tempstr != "")
        {
            tempstr = tempstr + ",";
        }
        tempstr = tempstr + (char)34 + row[col.Caption].ToString() + (char)34;
    }
    txtstream.WriteLine(tempstr);
    tempstr = "";

}
txtstream.Close();

System.Diagnostics.Process.Start(Application.StartupPath +
"\\Products.csv");
```

XML FILES

BELOW ARE XML CODING EXAMPLES IN TEXT AND DOM NOTATION FOR ATTRIBUTE XML, ELEMENT XML, ELEMENT XML FOR XSL AND SCHEMA XML.

TEXT CREATED ATTRIBUTE XML

```
Scripting.FileSystemObject fso = new Scripting.FileSystemObject();
Scripting.TextStream txtstream = fso.OpenTextFile(Application.StartupPath +
"\\Products.xml",IOMode.ForWriting, true, Tristate.TristateUseDefault);
txtstream.WriteLine("<?xml version=\"1.0\" encoding=\"iso-8859-1\"?>");
txtstream.WriteLine("<data>");
foreach(System.Data.DataRow row in dv.Table.Rows)
{
    txtstream.WriteLine("<products>");
    foreach(System.Data.DataColumn col in dv.Table.Columns)
    {
        string tstr = "";
        tstr = "<property name =\"" + col.Caption + "\" ";
        tstr = tstr + " datatype = \"" + col.DataType.Name + "\" ";
        tstr = tstr + " length =\"" + row[col.Caption].ToString().Length + "\" ";
        tstr = tstr + " value =\"" + row[col.Caption] + "\"/>";
        txtstream.WriteLine(tstr);
    }
    txtstream.WriteLine("</products>");
}
txtstream.WriteLine("</data>");
txtstream.Close();
```

DOM CREATED ATTRIBUTE XML

```
XmlDocument xmldoc = new XmlDocument();
XmlProcessingInstruction    pi    =    xmldoc.CreateProcessingInstruction("xml",
"version='1.0' encoding='iso-8895-1'");
XmlNode oRoot = xmldoc.CreateElement("data");
xmldoc.AppendChild(pi);
foreach (System.Data.DataRow row in dv.Table.Rows)
{
    XmlNode oNode = xmldoc.CreateNode(XmlNodeType.Element, "Products", null);
    foreach (System.Data.DataColumn col in dv.Table.Columns)
    {
        XmlNode oNode1 = xmldoc.CreateNode(XmlNodeType.Element, "Property",
null);
        XmlAttribute oatt = xmldoc.CreateAttribute("Name");
        oatt.Value = col.Caption;
        oNode1.Attributes.SetNamedItem(oatt);
        oatt = xmldoc.CreateAttribute("datatype");
        oatt.Value = col.DataType.Name;
        oNode1.Attributes.SetNamedItem(oatt);
        oatt = xmldoc.CreateAttribute("size");
        oatt.Value = row[col.Caption].ToString().Length.ToString();
        oNode1.Attributes.SetNamedItem(oatt);
        oatt = xmldoc.CreateAttribute("value");
        oatt.Value = row[col.Caption].ToString();
        oNode1.Attributes.SetNamedItem(oatt);
        oNode.AppendChild(oNode1);
    }
    oRoot.AppendChild(oNode);
}
xmldoc.AppendChild(oRoot);
xmldoc.Save(Application.StartupPath + "\\Products.xml");
```

TEXT CREATED ELEMENT XML

```
Scripting.FileSystemObject fso = new Scripting.FileSystemObject();
Scripting.TextStream txtstream = fso.OpenTextFile(Application.StartupPath +
"\\Products.xml",IOMode.ForWriting, true, Tristate.TristateUseDefault);
txtstream.WriteLine("<?xml version=\"1.0\" encoding=\"iso-8859-1\"?>");
txtstream.WriteLine("<data>");
foreach(System.Data.DataRow row in dv.Table.Rows)
{
    txtstream.WriteLine("<products>");
    foreach(System.Data.DataColumn col in dv.Table.Columns)
    {
        string tstr = "";
        tstr = "<" + col.Caption + ">";
        tstr = tstr + row[col.Caption];
        tstr = tstr + "</" + col.Caption + ">";
        txtstream.WriteLine(tstr);
    }
    txtstream.WriteLine("</products>");
}
txtstream.WriteLine("</data>");
txtstream.Close();
```

DOM CREATE ELEMENT XML

```
XmlDocument xmldoc = new XmlDocument();
XmlProcessingInstruction pi = xmldoc.CreateProcessingInstruction("xml",
"version='1.0' encoding='iso-8895-1'");
XmlNode oRoot = xmldoc.CreateElement("data");
xmldoc.AppendChild(pi);
foreach (System.Data.DataRow row in dv.Table.Rows)
{
    XmlNode oNode = xmldoc.CreateNode(XmlNodeType.Element, "Products", null);
    foreach (System.Data.DataColumn col in dv.Table.Columns)
    {
        XmlNode oNode1 = xmldoc.CreateNode(XmlNodeType.Element, col.Caption,
null);
        oNode1.InnerText = row[col.Caption].ToString();
        oNode.AppendChild(oNode1);
    }
    oRoot.AppendChild(oNode);
}
xmldoc.AppendChild(oRoot);
xmldoc.Save(Application.StartupPath + "\\Products.xml");
```

TEXT CREATED ELEMENT XML FOR XLS

```
Scripting.FileSystemObject fso = new Scripting.FileSystemObject();
Scripting.TextStream  txtstream  =  fso.OpenTextFile(Application.StartupPath  +
"\\Products.xml",IOMode.ForWriting, true, Tristate.TristateUseDefault);
txtstream.WriteLine("<?xml version=\"1.0\" encoding=\"iso-8859-1\"?>");
txtstream.WriteLine("<?xml-stylesheet type='Text/xsl' href=\"Products.xsl\"?>");

txtstream.WriteLine("<data>");
foreach(System.Data.DataRow row in dv.Table.Rows)
{
    txtstream.WriteLine("<products>");
    foreach(System.Data.DataColumn col in dv.Table.Columns)
    {
        string tstr = "";
        tstr = "<" + col.Caption + ">";
        tstr = tstr + row[col.Caption].ToString();
        tstr = tstr + "</" + col.Caption + ">";
        txtstream.WriteLine(tstr);
    }
    txtstream.WriteLine("</products>");
}
txtstream.WriteLine("</data>");
txtstream.Close();
```

DOM CREATE ELEMENT XML FOR XSL

```
XmlDocument xmldoc = new XmlDocument();
XmlProcessingInstruction  pi  =  xmldoc.CreateProcessingInstruction("xml",
"version='1.0' encoding='iso-8895-1'");
XmlProcessingInstruction  pii  =  xmldoc.CreateProcessingInstruction("xml-
stylesheet", "type='text/xsl' href='Products.xsl'");
XmlNode oRoot = xmldoc.CreateElement("data");
xmldoc.AppendChild(pi);
xmldoc.AppendChild(pii);
foreach (System.Data.DataRow row in dv.Table.Rows)
{
    XmlNode oNode = xmldoc.CreateNode(XmlNodeType.Element, "Products", null);
    foreach (System.Data.DataColumn col in dv.Table.Columns)
```

```
        {
            XmlNode oNode1 = xmldoc.CreateNode(XmlNodeType.Element, col.Caption,
null);
            oNode1.InnerText = row[col.Caption].ToString();
            oNode.AppendChild(oNode1);
        }
        oRoot.AppendChild(oNode);
    }
    xmldoc.AppendChild(oRoot);
    xmldoc.Save(Application.StartupPath + "\\Products.xml");
```

TEXT CREATED SCHEMA XML

```
Scripting.FileSystemObject fso = new Scripting.FileSystemObject();
Scripting.TextStream txtstream = fso.OpenTextFile(Application.StartupPath +
"\\Products.xml",IOMode.ForWriting, true, Tristate.TristateUseDefault);
txtstream.WriteLine("<?xml version=\"1.0\" encoding=\"iso-8859-1\"?>");
txtstream.WriteLine("<data>");
foreach(System.Data.DataRow row in dv.Table.Rows)
{
    txtstream.WriteLine("<products>");
    foreach(System.Data.DataColumn col in dv.Table.Columns)
    {
        string tstr = "";
        tstr = "<" + col.Caption + ">";
        tstr = tstr + row[col.Caption];
        tstr = tstr + "</" + col.Caption + ">";
        txtstream.WriteLine(tstr);
    }
    txtstream.WriteLine("</products>");
}
txtstream.WriteLine("</data>");
txtstream.Close();

ADODB.Recordset rs = new ADODB.Recordset();
rs.ActiveConnection = "Provider=MSDAOSP; Data Source = MSXML2.DSOControl; ";
rs.Open(Application.StartupPath + "\\Products.xml");
rs.Save(Application.StartupPath + "\\ProductsSchema.xml");
```

DOM CREATED SCHEMA XML

```
XmlDocument xmldoc = new XmlDocument();
XmlProcessingInstruction pi = xmldoc.CreateProcessingInstruction("xml",
"version='1.0' encoding='iso-8895-1'");
XmlNode oRoot = xmldoc.CreateElement("data");
xmldoc.AppendChild(pi);
foreach (System.Data.DataRow row in dv.Table.Rows)
{
    XmlNode oNode = xmldoc.CreateNode(XmlNodeType.Element, "Products", null);
    foreach (System.Data.DataColumn col in dv.Table.Columns)
    {
        XmlNode oNode1 = xmldoc.CreateNode(XmlNodeType.Element, col.Caption,
null);
        oNode1.InnerText = row[col.Caption].ToString();
        oNode.AppendChild(oNode1);
    }
    oRoot.AppendChild(oNode);
}
xmldoc.AppendChild(oRoot);
xmldoc.Save(Application.StartupPath + "\\Products.xml");

ADODB.Recordset rs = new ADODB.Recordset();
rs.ActiveConnection = "Provider=MSDAOSP; Data Source = MSXML2.DSOControl; ";
rs.Open(Application.StartupPath + "\\Products.xml");
rs.Save(Application.StartupPath + "\\ProductsSchema.xml");
```

XSL FILES

B ELOW ARE EXAMPLES OF WHAT YOU CAN DO WITH XSL. Views include reports and tables and orientation is for multi-line horizontal, multi-line VERTICAL, single line horizontal and single line VERTICAL.

```
Scripting.FileSystemObject fso = new Scripting.FileSystemObject();
    Scripting.TextStream txtstream = fso.OpenTextFile(Application.StartupPath +
"\\Products.xsl",IOMode.ForWriting, True, Tristate.TristateUseDefault);
    txtstream.WriteLine("<?xml version='1.0' encoding='UTF-8'?>");
    txtstream.WriteLine("<xsl:stylesheet version='1.0'
xmlns:xsl='http://www.w3.org/1999/XSL/Transform'>");
    txtstream.WriteLine("<xsl:template match=\"/\">");
    txtstream.WriteLine("<html>");
    txtstream.WriteLine("<head>");
    txtstream.WriteLine("<title>Products</title>");
    txtstream.WriteLine("</head>");
    txtstream.WriteLine("<body>");
```

For Reports:

```
    txtstream.WriteLine("<table border=""0"" colspacing=""3""
colpadding=""3"">");
```

For Tables:

```
    txtstream.WriteLine("<table border=""1"" colspacing=""3""
colpadding=""3"">");
```

Single Line Horizontal

```
txtstream.WriteLine("<tr>");
foreach(System.Data.DataColumn col in dv.Table.Columns)
{
    txtstream.WriteLine("<th align='left' nowrap='true'>" + col.Caption +
"</th>");
}
txtstream.WriteLine("</tr>");
```

None

```
txtstream.WriteLine("<tr>");
foreach(System.Data.DataColumn col in dv.Table.Columns)
{
    txtstream.WriteLine("<td><xsl:value-of select=\"data/Products/" + col.Caption
+ "\"/></td>");
}
txtstream.WriteLine("</tr>");
```

Button

```
txtstream.WriteLine("<tr>");
foreach(System.Data.DataColumn col in dv.Table.Columns)
{
    txtstream.WriteLine("<td align='left' nowrap='true'><button
style='width:100%;'><xsl:value-of select=\"data/Products/" + col.Caption  +
"\"/></button></td>");
}
txtstream.WriteLine("</tr>");
```

Combobox

```
txtstream.WriteLine("<tr>");
foreach(System.Data.DataColumn col in dv.Table.Columns)
{
    txtstream.WriteLine("<td                                     align='left'
nowrap='true'><select><option><xsl:attribute        name='value'><xsl:value-of
```

```
select=\"data/Products/"   +   col.Caption     +   "\"/></xsl:attribute><xsl:value-of
select=""data/Products/" + col.Caption  + "\"/></option></select></td>");
   }
   txtstream.WriteLine("</tr>");
```

```
   txtstream.WriteLine("<tr>");
   foreach(System.Data.DataColumn col in dv.Table.Columns)
   {
      txtstream.WriteLine("<td       align='left'   nowrap='true'><div><xsl:value-of
select=\"data/Products/" + col.Caption  + "\"/></div></td>");
   }
   txtstream.WriteLine("</tr>");
```

```
   txtstream.WriteLine("<tr>");
   foreach(System.Data.DataColumn col in dv.Table.Columns)
   {
      txtstream.WriteLine("<td         align='left'   nowrap='true'><a    href='"   +
row[col.Caption].ToString()    +    "'><xsl:value-of    select=\"data/Products/"   +
col.Caption  + "\"/></a></td>");
   }
   txtstream.WriteLine("</tr>");
```

```
   txtstream.WriteLine("<tr>");
   foreach(System.Data.DataColumn col in dv.Table.Columns)
   {
      txtstream.WriteLine("<td              align='left'        nowrap='true'><select
multiple><option><xsl:attribute                    name='value'><xsl:value-of
select=\"data/Products/"   +   col.Caption     +   "\"/></xsl:attribute><xsl:value-of
select=\"data/Products/" + col.Caption  + "\"/></option></select></td>");
   }
   txtstream.WriteLine("</tr>");
```

```
txtstream.WriteLine("<tr>");
foreach(System.Data.DataColumn col in dv.Table.Columns)
{
    txtstream.WriteLine("<td      align='left'   nowrap='true'><span><xsl:value-of
select=\"data/Products/" + col.Caption  + "\"/></span></td>");
}
txtstream.WriteLine("</tr>");
```

```
txtstream.WriteLine("<tr>");
foreach(System.Data.DataColumn col in dv.Table.Columns)
{
    txtstream.WriteLine("<td  align='left' nowrap='true'><textarea><xsl:value-of
select=\"data/Products/" + col.Caption  + "\"/></textarea></td>");
}
txtstream.WriteLine("</tr>");
```

```
txtstream.WriteLine("<tr>");
foreach(System.Data.DataColumn col in dv.Table.Columns)
{
    txtstream.WriteLine("<td  align='left' nowrap='true'><input
type='text'><xsl:attribute name=""value""><xsl:value-of select=\"data/Products/"
+ col.Caption  + "\"/></xsl:attribute></input></td>");
}
txtstream.WriteLine("</tr>");
```

End code for each routine:

```
txtstream.WriteLine("</table>");
txtstream.WriteLine("</body>");
txtstream.WriteLine("</html>");
txtstream.WriteLine("</xsl:template>");
txtstream.WriteLine("</xsl:stylesheet>");
txtstream.Close();
```

Multi Line Horizontal

```
txtstream.WriteLine("<tr>");
foreach(System.Data.DataColumn col in dv.Table.Columns)
{
    txtstream.WriteLine("<th align='left' nowrap='true'>" + col.Caption +
"</th>");
}
txtstream.WriteLine("</tr>");
```

None

```
txtstream.WriteLine("<xsl:for-each select=\"data/products\">");
txtstream.WriteLine("<tr>");
foreach(System.Data.DataColumn col in dv.Table.Columns)
{
    txtstream.WriteLine("<td><xsl:value-of select=\"" + col.Caption  +
"\""/></td>");
}
txtstream.WriteLine("</tr>");
txtstream.WriteLine("</xsl:for-each>");
```

Button

```
txtstream.WriteLine("<xsl:for-each select=\"data/products\">");
txtstream.WriteLine("<tr>");
foreach(System.Data.DataColumn col in dv.Table.Columns)
{
    txtstream.WriteLine("<td align='left' nowrap='true'><button
style='width:100%;'><xsl:value-of select=\"" + col.Caption  +
"\"/></button></td>");
}
txtstream.WriteLine("</tr>");
txtstream.WriteLine("</xsl:for-each>");
```

Combobox

```
txtstream.WriteLine("<xsl:for-each select=\"data/products\">");
txtstream.WriteLine("<tr>");
foreach(System.Data.DataColumn col in dv.Table.Columns)
{
```

```
  txtstream.WriteLine("<td                                        align='left'
nowrap='true'><select><option><xsl:attribute              name='value'><xsl:value-of
select=\""    +  col.Caption   +   """/></xsl:attribute><xsl:value-of  select=\""  +
col.Caption  + "\"/></option></select></td>");
 }
 txtstream.WriteLine("</tr>");
 txtstream.WriteLine("</xsl:for-each>");
```

Div

```
 txtstream.WriteLine("<xsl:for-each select=\"data/products\">");
 txtstream.WriteLine("<tr>");
 foreach(System.Data.DataColumn col in dv.Table.Columns)
 {
  txtstream.WriteLine("<td        align='left'   nowrap='true'><div><xsl:value-of
select=\"" + col.Caption  + "\"/></div></td>");
 }
 txtstream.WriteLine("</tr>");
 txtstream.WriteLine("</xsl:for-each>");
```

Link

```
 txtstream.WriteLine("<xsl:for-each select=\"data/products\">");
 txtstream.WriteLine("<tr>");
 foreach(System.Data.DataColumn col in dv.Table.Columns)
 {
  txtstream.WriteLine("<td        align='left'   nowrap='true'><a       href='"    +
row[col.Caption].ToString()   +   "'><xsl:value-of   select=\""   +   col.Caption    +
"\"/></a></td>");
 }
 txtstream.WriteLine("</tr>");
 txtstream.WriteLine("</xsl:for-each>");
```

Listbox

```
 txtstream.WriteLine("<xsl:for-each select=\"data/products\">");
 txtstream.WriteLine("<tr>");
 foreach(System.Data.DataColumn col in dv.Table.Columns)
 {
  txtstream.WriteLine("<td                align='left'        nowrap='true'><select
multiple><option><xsl:attribute     name='value'><xsl:value-of      select=\""     +
```

```
col.Caption    +   "\"/></xsl:attribute><xsl:value-of  select=\""  +  col.Caption    +
"\"/></option></select></td>");
    }
    txtstream.WriteLine("</tr>");
```

```
    txtstream.WriteLine("<xsl:for-each select=\"data/products\">");
    txtstream.WriteLine("<tr>");
    foreach(System.Data.DataColumn col in dv.Table.Columns)
    {
        txtstream.WriteLine("<td      align='left'  nowrap='true'><span><xsl:value-of
select=\"" + col.Caption  + "\"/></span></td>");
    }
    txtstream.WriteLine("</tr>");
    txtstream.WriteLine("</xsl:for-each>");
```

textarea

```
    txtstream.WriteLine("<xsl:for-each select=\"data/products\">");
    txtstream.WriteLine("<tr>");
    foreach(System.Data.DataColumn col in dv.Table.Columns)
    {
        txtstream.WriteLine("<td align='left' nowrap='true'><textarea><xsl:value-of
select=\"" + col.Caption  + "\"/></textarea></td>");
    }
    txtstream.WriteLine("</tr>");
    txtstream.WriteLine("</xsl:for-each>");
```

Textbox

```
    txtstream.WriteLine("<xsl:for-each select=\"data/products\">");
    txtstream.WriteLine("<tr>");
    foreach(System.Data.DataColumn col in dv.Table.Columns)
    {
        txtstream.WriteLine("<td align='left' nowrap='true'><input
type='text'><xsl:attribute name=\"value\"><xsl:value-of select=\"" + col.Caption  +
"\"/></xsl:attribute></input></td>");
    }
    txtstream.WriteLine("</tr>");
    txtstream.WriteLine("</xsl:for-each>");
```

End Code for Each routine.

```
txtstream.WriteLine("</table>");
txtstream.WriteLine("</body>");
txtstream.WriteLine("</html>");
txtstream.WriteLine("</xsl:template>");
txtstream.WriteLine("</xsl:stylesheet>");
txtstream.Close();
```

Single Line VERTICAL

```
foreach(System.Data.DataColumn col in dv.Table.Columns)
{
    txtstream.WriteLine("<tr><th align='left' nowrap='true'>" + col.Caption +
"</th>");
```

None

```
    txtstream.WriteLine("<td><xsl:value-of select=\"data/Products/" + col.Caption
+ "\"/></td></tr>");
```

Button

```
    txtstream.WriteLine("<td align='left' nowrap='true'><button
style='width:100%;'><xsl:value-of select=\"data/Products/" + col.Caption +
"\"/></button></td></tr>");
```

Combobox

```
    txtstream.WriteLine("<td                                    align='left'
nowrap='true'><select><option><xsl:attribute            name='value'><xsl:value-of
select=\"data/Products/"    +    col.Caption    +    "\"/></xsl:attribute><xsl:value-of
select=""data/Products/" + col.Caption  + "\"/></option></select></td></tr>");
```

Div

```
    txtstream.WriteLine("<td       align='left'    nowrap='true'><div><xsl:value-of
select=\"data/Products/" + col.Caption  + "\"/></div></td></tr>");
```

Link

```
txtstream.WriteLine("<td        align='left'    nowrap='true'><a    href='"    +
row[col.Caption].ToString()    +    "'><xsl:value-of    select=\"data/Products/"    +
col.Caption  +  "\"/></a></td></tr>");
```

Listbox

```
txtstream.WriteLine("<td              align='left'        nowrap='true'><select
multiple><option><xsl:attribute                    name='value'><xsl:value-of
select=\"data/Products/"   +   col.Caption     +    "\"/></xsl:attribute><xsl:value-of
select=\"data/Products/"  +  col.Caption  +  "\"/></option></select></td></tr>");
```

Span

```
txtstream.WriteLine("<td       align='left'   nowrap='true'><span><xsl:value-of
select=\"data/Products/" + col.Caption  +  "\"/></span></td></tr>");
```

textarea

```
txtstream.WriteLine("<td  align='left'  nowrap='true'><textarea><xsl:value-of
select=\"data/Products/" + col.Caption  +  "\"/></textarea></td></tr>");
```

Textbox

```
txtstream.WriteLine("<td  align='left'  nowrap='true'><input
type='text'><xsl:attribute name=""value""><xsl:value-of select=\"data/Products/"
+ col.Caption  +  "\"/></xsl:attribute></input></td></tr>");
```


End Code for Each routine.

```
    }
    txtstream.WriteLine("</table>");
    txtstream.WriteLine("</body>");
    txtstream.WriteLine("</html>");
    txtstream.WriteLine("</xsl:template>");
    txtstream.WriteLine("</xsl:stylesheet>");
    txtstream.Close();
```

Multi Line VERTICAL

```
foreach(System.Data.DataColumn col in dv.Table.Columns)
{
    txtstream.WriteLine("<tr><th align='left' nowrap='true'>" + col.Caption +
"</th>");
```

None

```
    txtstream.WriteLine("<xsl:for-each select=\"data/products\">");
    foreach(System.Data.DataColumn col in dv.Table.Columns)
    {
        txtstream.WriteLine("<td><xsl:value-of select=\"" + col.Caption +
"\""/></td>");
    }
    txtstream.WriteLine("</xsl:for-each>")
    txtstream.WriteLine("</tr>");
```

Button

```
    txtstream.WriteLine("<xsl:for-each select=\"data/products\">");
    foreach(System.Data.DataColumn col in dv.Table.Columns)
    {
        txtstream.WriteLine("<td align='left' nowrap='true'><button
style='width:100%;'><xsl:value-of select=\"" + col.Caption +
"\"/></button></td>");
    }
    txtstream.WriteLine("</tr>");
    txtstream.WriteLine("</xsl:for-each>");
```

Combobox

```
    txtstream.WriteLine("<xsl:for-each select=\"data/products\">");
    foreach(System.Data.DataColumn col in dv.Table.Columns)
    {
        txtstream.WriteLine("<td                                align='left'
nowrap='true'><select><option><xsl:attribute         name='value'><xsl:value-of
select=\"" + col.Caption + "\""/></xsl:attribute><xsl:value-of select=\"" +
col.Caption + "\"/></option></select></td>");
    }
    txtstream.WriteLine("</tr>");
    txtstream.WriteLine("</xsl:for-each>");
```

Div

```
txtstream.WriteLine("<xsl:for-each select=\"data/products\">");
foreach(System.Data.DataColumn col in dv.Table.Columns)
{
    txtstream.WriteLine("<td        align='left'    nowrap='true'><div><xsl:value-of
select=\"" + col.Caption  + "\"/></div></td>");
}
txtstream.WriteLine("</xsl:for-each>");
txtstream.WriteLine("</tr>");
```

Link

```
txtstream.WriteLine("<xsl:for-each select=\"data/products\">");
foreach(System.Data.DataColumn col in dv.Table.Columns)
{
    txtstream.WriteLine("<td        align='left'   nowrap='true'><a   href='"   +
row[col.Caption].ToString()   +   "'><xsl:value-of   select=\""   +   col.Caption   +
"\"/></a></td>");
}
txtstream.WriteLine("</tr>");
txtstream.WriteLine("</xsl:for-each>");
```

Listbox

```
txtstream.WriteLine("<xsl:for-each select=\"data/products\">");
foreach(System.Data.DataColumn col in dv.Table.Columns)
{
    txtstream.WriteLine("<td            align='left'       nowrap='true'><select
multiple><option><xsl:attribute    name='value'><xsl:value-of    select=\""    +
col.Caption    +   "\"/></xsl:attribute><xsl:value-of   select=\""   +   col.Caption   +
"\"/></option></select></td>");
}
txtstream.WriteLine("</xsl:for-each>");
txtstream.WriteLine("</tr>");
```

Span

```
txtstream.WriteLine("<xsl:for-each select=\"data/products\">");
foreach(System.Data.DataColumn col in dv.Table.Columns)
{
```

```
    txtstream.WriteLine("<td        align='left'   nowrap='true'><span><xsl:value-of
select=\"" + col.Caption  + "\"/></span></td>");
    }
  txtstream.WriteLine("</xsl:for-each>");
  txtstream.WriteLine("</tr>");
```

textarea

```
  txtstream.WriteLine("<xsl:for-each select=\"data/products\">");
  foreach(System.Data.DataColumn col in dv.Table.Columns)
  {
    txtstream.WriteLine("<td align='left' nowrap='true'><textarea><xsl:value-of
select=\"" + col.Caption  + "\"/></textarea></td>");
    }
  txtstream.WriteLine("</xsl:for-each>");
  txtstream.WriteLine("</tr>");
```

Textbox

```
  txtstream.WriteLine("<xsl:for-each select=\"data/products\">");

  foreach(System.Data.DataColumn col in dv.Table.Columns)
  {
    txtstream.WriteLine("<td  align='left' nowrap='true'><input
type='text'><xsl:attribute name=\"value\"><xsl:value-of select=\"" + col.Caption  +
"\"/></xsl:attribute></input></td>");
    }
  txtstream.WriteLine("</xsl:for-each>");
  txtstream.WriteLine("</tr>");
```

End Code for Each routine.

```
  txtstream.WriteLine("</table>");
  txtstream.WriteLine("</body>");
  txtstream.WriteLine("</html>");
  txtstream.WriteLine("</xsl:template>");
  txtstream.WriteLine("</xsl:stylesheet>");
  txtstream.Close();
```

STYLESHEETS

Fuel for Thought

T HESE ARE SUPPLIED AS IS AND ARE JUST SOME IDEAS I THINK YOU WILL LIKE. DON'T SHOOT THE MESSANGER.

None

```
txtstream.WriteLine("<style type='text/css'>");
txtstream.WriteLine("th");
txtstream.WriteLine("{");
txtstream.WriteLine("   COLOR: white;");
txtstream.WriteLine("}");
txtstream.WriteLine("td");
txtstream.WriteLine("{");
txtstream.WriteLine("   COLOR: white;");
txtstream.WriteLine("}");
txtstream.WriteLine("</style>");
```

Its A Table

```
txtstream.WriteLine("<style type='text/css'>");
txtstream.WriteLine("#itsthetable {");
txtstream.WriteLine("      font-family: Georgia, """"Times New Roman"""",
Times, serif;");
txtstream.WriteLine("      color: #036;");
txtstream.WriteLine("}");

txtstream.WriteLine("caption {");
```

```
txtstream.WriteLine("      font-size: 48px;");
txtstream.WriteLine("      color: #036;");
txtstream.WriteLine("      font-weight: bolder;");
txtstream.WriteLine("      font-variant: small-caps;");
txtstream.WriteLine("}");

txtstream.WriteLine("th {");
txtstream.WriteLine("      font-size: 12px;");
txtstream.WriteLine("      color: #FFF;");
txtstream.WriteLine("      background-color: #06C;");
txtstream.WriteLine("      padding: 8px 4px;");
txtstream.WriteLine("      border-bottom: 1px solid #015ebc;");
txtstream.WriteLine("}");

txtstream.WriteLine("table {");
txtstream.WriteLine("      margin: 0;");
txtstream.WriteLine("      padding: 0;");
txtstream.WriteLine("      border-collapse: collapse;");
txtstream.WriteLine("      border: 1px solid #06C;");
txtstream.WriteLine("      width: 100%");
txtstream.WriteLine("}");

txtstream.WriteLine("#itsthetable th a:link, #itsthetable th a:visited {");
txtstream.WriteLine("      color: #FFF;");
txtstream.WriteLine("      text-decoration: none;");
txtstream.WriteLine("      border-left: 5px solid #FFF;");
txtstream.WriteLine("      padding-left: 3px;");
txtstream.WriteLine("}");

txtstream.WriteLine("th a:hover, #itsthetable th a:active {");
txtstream.WriteLine("      color: #F90;");
txtstream.WriteLine("      text-decoration: line-through;");
txtstream.WriteLine("      border-left: 5px solid #F90;");
txtstream.WriteLine("      padding-left: 3px;");
txtstream.WriteLine("}");

txtstream.WriteLine("tbody th:hover {");
txtstream.WriteLine("      background-image: url(imgs/tbody_hover.gif);");
txtstream.WriteLine("      background-position: bottom;");
txtstream.WriteLine("      background-repeat: repeat-x;");
txtstream.WriteLine("}");

txtstream.WriteLine("td {");
txtstream.WriteLine("      background-color: #f2f2f2;");
txtstream.WriteLine("      padding: 4px;");
txtstream.WriteLine("      font-size: 12px;");
txtstream.WriteLine("}");

txtstream.WriteLine("#itsthetable td:hover {");
txtstream.WriteLine("      background-color: #f8f8f8;");
```

```
txtstream.WriteLine("}");

txtstream.WriteLine("#itsthetable td a:link, #itsthetable td a:visited {");
txtstream.WriteLine("    color: #039;");
txtstream.WriteLine("    text-decoration: none;");
txtstream.WriteLine("    border-left: 3px solid #039;");
txtstream.WriteLine("    padding-left: 3px;");
txtstream.WriteLine("}");

txtstream.WriteLine("#itsthetable td a:hover, #itsthetable td a:active {");
txtstream.WriteLine("    color: #06C;");
txtstream.WriteLine("    text-decoration: line-through;");
txtstream.WriteLine("    border-left: 3px solid #06C;");
txtstream.WriteLine("    padding-left: 3px;");
txtstream.WriteLine("}");

txtstream.WriteLine("#itsthetable th {");
txtstream.WriteLine("    text-align: left;");
txtstream.WriteLine("    width: 150px;");
txtstream.WriteLine("}");

txtstream.WriteLine("#itsthetable tr {");
txtstream.WriteLine("    border-bottom: 1px solid #CCC;");
txtstream.WriteLine("}");

txtstream.WriteLine("#itsthetable thead th {");
txtstream.WriteLine("    background-image: url(imgs/thead_back.gif);");
txtstream.WriteLine("    background-repeat: repeat-x;");
txtstream.WriteLine("    background-color: #06C;");
txtstream.WriteLine("    height: 30px;");
txtstream.WriteLine("    font-size: 18px;");
txtstream.WriteLine("    text-align: center;");
txtstream.WriteLine("    text-shadow: #333 2px 2px;");
txtstream.WriteLine("    border: 2px;");
txtstream.WriteLine("}");

txtstream.WriteLine("#itsthetable tfoot th {");
txtstream.WriteLine("    background-image: url(imgs/tfoot_back.gif);");
txtstream.WriteLine("    background-repeat: repeat-x;");
txtstream.WriteLine("    background-color: #036;");
txtstream.WriteLine("    height: 30px;");
txtstream.WriteLine("    font-size: 28px;");
txtstream.WriteLine("    text-align: center;");
txtstream.WriteLine("    text-shadow: #333 2px 2px;");
txtstream.WriteLine("}");

txtstream.WriteLine("#itsthetable tfoot td {");
txtstream.WriteLine("    background-image: url(imgs/tfoot_back.gif);");
txtstream.WriteLine("    background-repeat: repeat-x;");
```

```
txtstream.WriteLine("        background-color: #036;");
txtstream.WriteLine("        color: FFF;");
txtstream.WriteLine("        height: 30px;");
txtstream.WriteLine("        font-size: 24px;");
txtstream.WriteLine("        text-align: left;");
txtstream.WriteLine("        text-shadow: #333 2px 2px;");
txtstream.WriteLine("}");

txtstream.WriteLine("tbody td a[href=""""""http://www.csslab.cl/""""""] {");
txtstream.WriteLine("        font-weight: bolder;");
txtstream.WriteLine("}");
txtstream.WriteLine("</style>");
```

Black and White Text

```
txtstream.WriteLine("<style type='text/css'>");
txtstream.WriteLine("th");
txtstream.WriteLine("{");
txtstream.WriteLine("   COLOR: white;");
txtstream.WriteLine("   BACKGROUND-COLOR: black;");
txtstream.WriteLine("   FONT-FAMILY: Cambria, serif;");
txtstream.WriteLine("   FONT-SIZE: 12px;");
txtstream.WriteLine("   text-align: left;");
txtstream.WriteLine("   white-Space: nowrap='nowrap';");
txtstream.WriteLine("}");
txtstream.WriteLine("td");
txtstream.WriteLine("{");
txtstream.WriteLine("   COLOR: white;");
txtstream.WriteLine("   BACKGROUND-COLOR: black;");
txtstream.WriteLine("   FONT-FAMILY:  Cambria, serif;");
txtstream.WriteLine("   FONT-SIZE: 12px;");
txtstream.WriteLine("   text-align: left;");
txtstream.WriteLine("   white-Space: nowrap='nowrap';");
txtstream.WriteLine("}");
txtstream.WriteLine("div");
txtstream.WriteLine("{");
txtstream.WriteLine("   COLOR: white;");
txtstream.WriteLine("   BACKGROUND-COLOR: black;");
txtstream.WriteLine("   FONT-FAMILY:  Cambria, serif;");
txtstream.WriteLine("   FONT-SIZE: 10px;");
txtstream.WriteLine("   text-align: left;");
txtstream.WriteLine("   white-Space: nowrap='nowrap';");
txtstream.WriteLine("}");
txtstream.WriteLine("span");
txtstream.WriteLine("{");
txtstream.WriteLine("   COLOR: white;");
txtstream.WriteLine("   BACKGROUND-COLOR: black;");
txtstream.WriteLine("   FONT-FAMILY:  Cambria, serif;");
```

```
txtstream.WriteLine("    FONT-SIZE: 10px;");
txtstream.WriteLine("    text-align: left;");
txtstream.WriteLine("    white-Space: nowrap='nowrap';");
txtstream.WriteLine("    display:inline-block;");
txtstream.WriteLine("    width: 100%;");
txtstream.WriteLine("}");
txtstream.WriteLine("textarea");
txtstream.WriteLine("{");
txtstream.WriteLine("    COLOR: white;");
txtstream.WriteLine("    BACKGROUND-COLOR: black;");
txtstream.WriteLine("    FONT-FAMILY: Cambria, serif;");
txtstream.WriteLine("    FONT-SIZE: 10px;");
txtstream.WriteLine("    text-align: left;");
txtstream.WriteLine("    white-Space: nowrap='nowrap';");
txtstream.WriteLine("    width: 100%;");
txtstream.WriteLine("}");
txtstream.WriteLine("select");
txtstream.WriteLine("{");
txtstream.WriteLine("    COLOR: white;");
txtstream.WriteLine("    BACKGROUND-COLOR: black;");
txtstream.WriteLine("    FONT-FAMILY: Cambria, serif;");
txtstream.WriteLine("    FONT-SIZE: 10px;");
txtstream.WriteLine("    text-align: left;");
txtstream.WriteLine("    white-Space: nowrap='nowrap';");
txtstream.WriteLine("    width: 100%;");
txtstream.WriteLine("}");
txtstream.WriteLine("input");
txtstream.WriteLine("{");
txtstream.WriteLine("    COLOR: white;");
txtstream.WriteLine("    BACKGROUND-COLOR: black;");
txtstream.WriteLine("    FONT-FAMILY: Cambria, serif;");
txtstream.WriteLine("    FONT-SIZE: 12px;");
txtstream.WriteLine("    text-align: left;");
txtstream.WriteLine("    display:table-cell;");
txtstream.WriteLine("    white-Space: nowrap='nowrap';");
txtstream.WriteLine("}");
txtstream.WriteLine("h1 {");
txtstream.WriteLine("color: antiquewhite;");
txtstream.WriteLine("text-shadow: 1px 1px 1px black;");
txtstream.WriteLine("padding: 3px;");
txtstream.WriteLine("text-align: center;");
txtstream.WriteLine("box-shadow: inset 2px 2px 5px rgba(0,0,0,0.5), inset -2px -2px 5px rgba(255,255,255,0.5);");
txtstream.WriteLine("}");
txtstream.WriteLine("</style>");
```

Colored Text

```
txtstream.WriteLine("<style type='text/css'>");
txtstream.WriteLine("th");
txtstream.WriteLine("{");
txtstream.WriteLine("    COLOR: darkred;");
txtstream.WriteLine("    BACKGROUND-COLOR: #eeeeee;");
txtstream.WriteLine("    FONT-FAMILY: Cambria, serif;");
txtstream.WriteLine("    FONT-SIZE: 12px;");
txtstream.WriteLine("    text-align: left;");
txtstream.WriteLine("    white-Space: nowrap='nowrap';");
txtstream.WriteLine("}");
txtstream.WriteLine("td");
txtstream.WriteLine("{");
txtstream.WriteLine("    COLOR: navy;");
txtstream.WriteLine("    BACKGROUND-COLOR: #eeeeee;");
txtstream.WriteLine("    FONT-FAMILY: Cambria, serif;");
txtstream.WriteLine("    FONT-SIZE: 12px;");
txtstream.WriteLine("    text-align: left;");
txtstream.WriteLine("    white-Space: nowrap='nowrap';");
txtstream.WriteLine("}");
txtstream.WriteLine("div");
txtstream.WriteLine("{");
txtstream.WriteLine("    COLOR: white;");
txtstream.WriteLine("    BACKGROUND-COLOR: navy;");
txtstream.WriteLine("    FONT-FAMILY: Cambria, serif;");
txtstream.WriteLine("    FONT-SIZE: 10px;");
txtstream.WriteLine("    text-align: left;");
txtstream.WriteLine("    white-Space: nowrap='nowrap';");
txtstream.WriteLine("}");
txtstream.WriteLine("span");
txtstream.WriteLine("{");
txtstream.WriteLine("    COLOR: white;");
txtstream.WriteLine("    BACKGROUND-COLOR: navy;");
txtstream.WriteLine("    FONT-FAMILY: Cambria, serif;");
txtstream.WriteLine("    FONT-SIZE: 10px;");
txtstream.WriteLine("    text-align: left;");
txtstream.WriteLine("    white-Space: nowrap='nowrap';");
txtstream.WriteLine("    display:inline-block;");
txtstream.WriteLine("    width: 100%;");
txtstream.WriteLine("}");
txtstream.WriteLine("textarea");
txtstream.WriteLine("{");
txtstream.WriteLine("    COLOR: white;");
txtstream.WriteLine("    BACKGROUND-COLOR: navy;");
txtstream.WriteLine("    FONT-FAMILY: Cambria, serif;");
txtstream.WriteLine("    FONT-SIZE: 10px;");
txtstream.WriteLine("    text-align: left;");
txtstream.WriteLine("    white-Space: nowrap='nowrap';");
txtstream.WriteLine("    width: 100%;");
txtstream.WriteLine("}");
txtstream.WriteLine("select");
```

```
txtstream.WriteLine("{");
txtstream.WriteLine("    COLOR: white;");
txtstream.WriteLine("    BACKGROUND-COLOR: navy;");
txtstream.WriteLine("    FONT-FAMILY: Cambria, serif;");
txtstream.WriteLine("    FONT-SIZE: 10px;");
txtstream.WriteLine("    text-align: left;");
txtstream.WriteLine("    white-Space: nowrap='nowrap';");
txtstream.WriteLine("    width: 100%;");
txtstream.WriteLine("}");
txtstream.WriteLine("input");
txtstream.WriteLine("{");
txtstream.WriteLine("    COLOR: white;");
txtstream.WriteLine("    BACKGROUND-COLOR: navy;");
txtstream.WriteLine("    FONT-FAMILY: Cambria, serif;");
txtstream.WriteLine("    FONT-SIZE: 12px;");
txtstream.WriteLine("    text-align: left;");
txtstream.WriteLine("    display:table-cell;");
txtstream.WriteLine("    white-Space: nowrap='nowrap';");
txtstream.WriteLine("}");
txtstream.WriteLine("h1 {");
txtstream.WriteLine("color: antiquewhite;");
txtstream.WriteLine("text-shadow: 1px 1px 1px black;");
txtstream.WriteLine("padding: 3px;");
txtstream.WriteLine("text-align: center;");
txtstream.WriteLine("box-shadow: inset 2px 2px 5px rgba(0,0,0,0.5), inset -2px -
2px 5px rgba(255,255,255,0.5);");
txtstream.WriteLine("}");
txtstream.WriteLine("</style>");
```

Oscillating Row Colors

```
txtstream.WriteLine("<style type='text/css'>");
txtstream.WriteLine("th");
txtstream.WriteLine("{");
txtstream.WriteLine("    COLOR: white;");
txtstream.WriteLine("    BACKGROUND-COLOR: navy;");
txtstream.WriteLine("    FONT-FAMILY: Cambria, serif;");
txtstream.WriteLine("    FONT-SIZE: 12px;");
txtstream.WriteLine("    text-align: left;");
txtstream.WriteLine("    white-Space: nowrap='nowrap';");
txtstream.WriteLine("}");
txtstream.WriteLine("td");
txtstream.WriteLine("{");
txtstream.WriteLine("    COLOR: navy;");
txtstream.WriteLine("    FONT-FAMILY: Cambria, serif;");
txtstream.WriteLine("    FONT-SIZE: 12px;");
txtstream.WriteLine("    text-align: left;");
```

```
txtstream.WriteLine("    white-Space: nowrap='nowrap';");
txtstream.WriteLine("}");
txtstream.WriteLine("div");
txtstream.WriteLine("{");
txtstream.WriteLine("    COLOR: navy;");
txtstream.WriteLine("    FONT-FAMILY: Cambria, serif;");
txtstream.WriteLine("    FONT-SIZE: 12px;");
txtstream.WriteLine("    text-align: left;");
txtstream.WriteLine("    white-Space: nowrap='nowrap';");
txtstream.WriteLine("}");
txtstream.WriteLine("span");
txtstream.WriteLine("{");
txtstream.WriteLine("    COLOR: navy;");
txtstream.WriteLine("    FONT-FAMILY: Cambria, serif;");
txtstream.WriteLine("    FONT-SIZE: 12px;");
txtstream.WriteLine("    text-align: left;");
txtstream.WriteLine("    white-Space: nowrap='nowrap';");
txtstream.WriteLine("    width: 100%;");
txtstream.WriteLine("}");
txtstream.WriteLine("textarea");
txtstream.WriteLine("{");
txtstream.WriteLine("    COLOR: navy;");
txtstream.WriteLine("    FONT-FAMILY: Cambria, serif;");
txtstream.WriteLine("    FONT-SIZE: 12px;");
txtstream.WriteLine("    text-align: left;");
txtstream.WriteLine("    white-Space: nowrap='nowrap';");
txtstream.WriteLine("    display:inline-block;");
txtstream.WriteLine("    width: 100%;");
txtstream.WriteLine("}");
txtstream.WriteLine("select");
txtstream.WriteLine("{");
txtstream.WriteLine("    COLOR: navy;");
txtstream.WriteLine("    FONT-FAMILY: Cambria, serif;");
txtstream.WriteLine("    FONT-SIZE: 10px;");
txtstream.WriteLine("    text-align: left;");
txtstream.WriteLine("    white-Space: nowrap='nowrap';");
txtstream.WriteLine("    display:inline-block;");
txtstream.WriteLine("    width: 100%;");
txtstream.WriteLine("}");
txtstream.WriteLine("input");
txtstream.WriteLine("{");
txtstream.WriteLine("    COLOR: navy;");
txtstream.WriteLine("    FONT-FAMILY: Cambria, serif;");
txtstream.WriteLine("    FONT-SIZE: 12px;");
txtstream.WriteLine("    text-align: left;");
txtstream.WriteLine("    display:table-cell;");
txtstream.WriteLine("    white-Space: nowrap='nowrap';");
txtstream.WriteLine("}");
txtstream.WriteLine("h1 {");
txtstream.WriteLine("color: antiquewhite;");
```

```
txtstream.WriteLine("text-shadow: 1px 1px 1px black;");
txtstream.WriteLine("padding: 3px;");
txtstream.WriteLine("text-align: center;");
txtstream.WriteLine("box-shadow: inset 2px 2px 5px rgba(0,0,0,0.5), inset -2px -
2px 5px rgba(255,255,255,0.5);");
txtstream.WriteLine("}");
txtstream.WriteLine("tr:nth-child(even){background-color:#f2f2f2;}");
txtstream.WriteLine("tr:nth-child(odd){background-color:#cccccc;
color:#f2f2f2;}");
txtstream.WriteLine("</style>");
```

Ghost Decorated

```
txtstream.WriteLine("<style type='text/css'>");
txtstream.WriteLine("th");
txtstream.WriteLine("{");
txtstream.WriteLine("    COLOR: black;");
txtstream.WriteLine("    BACKGROUND-COLOR: white;");
txtstream.WriteLine("    FONT-FAMILY: Cambria, serif;");
txtstream.WriteLine("    FONT-SIZE: 12px;");
txtstream.WriteLine("    text-align: left;");
txtstream.WriteLine("    white-Space: nowrap='nowrap';");
txtstream.WriteLine("}");
txtstream.WriteLine("td");
txtstream.WriteLine("{");
txtstream.WriteLine("    COLOR: black;");
txtstream.WriteLine("    BACKGROUND-COLOR: white;");
txtstream.WriteLine("    FONT-FAMILY: Cambria, serif;");
txtstream.WriteLine("    FONT-SIZE: 12px;");
txtstream.WriteLine("    text-align: left;");
txtstream.WriteLine("    white-Space: nowrap='nowrap';");
txtstream.WriteLine("}");
txtstream.WriteLine("div");
txtstream.WriteLine("{");
txtstream.WriteLine("    COLOR: black;");
txtstream.WriteLine("    BACKGROUND-COLOR: white;");
txtstream.WriteLine("    FONT-FAMILY: Cambria, serif;");
txtstream.WriteLine("    FONT-SIZE: 10px;");
txtstream.WriteLine("    text-align: left;");
txtstream.WriteLine("    white-Space: nowrap='nowrap';");
txtstream.WriteLine("}");
txtstream.WriteLine("span");
txtstream.WriteLine("{");
txtstream.WriteLine("    COLOR: black;");
txtstream.WriteLine("    BACKGROUND-COLOR: white;");
txtstream.WriteLine("    FONT-FAMILY: Cambria, serif;");
txtstream.WriteLine("    FONT-SIZE: 10px;");
txtstream.WriteLine("    text-align: left;");
txtstream.WriteLine("    white-Space: nowrap='nowrap';");
```

```
txtstream.WriteLine("    display:inline-block;");
txtstream.WriteLine("    width: 100%;");
txtstream.WriteLine("}");
txtstream.WriteLine("textarea");
txtstream.WriteLine("{");
txtstream.WriteLine("    COLOR: black;");
txtstream.WriteLine("    BACKGROUND-COLOR: white;");
txtstream.WriteLine("    FONT-FAMILY: Cambria, serif;");
txtstream.WriteLine("    FONT-SIZE: 10px;");
txtstream.WriteLine("    text-align: left;");
txtstream.WriteLine("    white-Space: nowrap='nowrap';");
txtstream.WriteLine("    width: 100%;");
txtstream.WriteLine("}");
txtstream.WriteLine("select");
txtstream.WriteLine("{");
txtstream.WriteLine("    COLOR: black;");
txtstream.WriteLine("    BACKGROUND-COLOR: white;");
txtstream.WriteLine("    FONT-FAMILY: Cambria, serif;");
txtstream.WriteLine("    FONT-SIZE: 10px;");
txtstream.WriteLine("    text-align: left;");
txtstream.WriteLine("    white-Space: nowrap='nowrap';");
txtstream.WriteLine("    width: 100%;");
txtstream.WriteLine("}");
txtstream.WriteLine("input");
txtstream.WriteLine("{");
txtstream.WriteLine("    COLOR: black;");
txtstream.WriteLine("    BACKGROUND-COLOR: white;");
txtstream.WriteLine("    FONT-FAMILY: Cambria, serif;");
txtstream.WriteLine("    FONT-SIZE: 12px;");
txtstream.WriteLine("    text-align: left;");
txtstream.WriteLine("    display:table-cell;");
txtstream.WriteLine("    white-Space: nowrap='nowrap';");
txtstream.WriteLine("}");
txtstream.WriteLine("h1 {");
txtstream.WriteLine("color: antiquewhite;");
txtstream.WriteLine("text-shadow: 1px 1px 1px black;");
txtstream.WriteLine("padding: 3px;");
txtstream.WriteLine("text-align: center;");
txtstream.WriteLine("box-shadow: inset 2px 2px 5px rgba(0,0,0,0.5), inset -2px -
2px 5px rgba(255,255,255,0.5);");
txtstream.WriteLine("}");
txtstream.WriteLine("</style>");
```

3D

```
txtstream.WriteLine("<style type='text/css'>");
txtstream.WriteLine("body");
txtstream.WriteLine("{");
txtstream.WriteLine("    PADDING-RIGHT: 0px;");
```

```
txtstream.WriteLine("    PADDING-LEFT: 0px;");
txtstream.WriteLine("    PADDING-BOTTOM: 0px;");
txtstream.WriteLine("    MARGIN: 0px;");
txtstream.WriteLine("    COLOR: #333;");
txtstream.WriteLine("    PADDING-TOP: 0px;");
txtstream.WriteLine("    FONT-FAMILY: verdana, arial, helvetica, sans-serif;");
txtstream.WriteLine("}");
txtstream.WriteLine("table");
txtstream.WriteLine("{");
txtstream.WriteLine("    BORDER-RIGHT: #999999 3px solid;");
txtstream.WriteLine("    PADDING-RIGHT: 6px;");
txtstream.WriteLine("    PADDING-LEFT: 6px;");
txtstream.WriteLine("    FONT-WEIGHT: Bold;");
txtstream.WriteLine("    FONT-SIZE: 14px;");
txtstream.WriteLine("    PADDING-BOTTOM: 6px;");
txtstream.WriteLine("    COLOR: Peru;");
txtstream.WriteLine("    LINE-HEIGHT: 14px;");
txtstream.WriteLine("    PADDING-TOP: 6px;");
txtstream.WriteLine("    BORDER-BOTTOM: #999 1px solid;");
txtstream.WriteLine("    BACKGROUND-COLOR: #eeeeee;");
txtstream.WriteLine("    FONT-FAMILY: verdana, arial, helvetica, sans-serif;");
txtstream.WriteLine("    FONT-SIZE: 12px;");
txtstream.WriteLine("}");
txtstream.WriteLine("th");
txtstream.WriteLine("{");
txtstream.WriteLine("    BORDER-RIGHT: #999999 3px solid;");
txtstream.WriteLine("    PADDING-RIGHT: 6px;");
txtstream.WriteLine("    PADDING-LEFT: 6px;");
txtstream.WriteLine("    FONT-WEIGHT: Bold;");
txtstream.WriteLine("    FONT-SIZE: 14px;");
txtstream.WriteLine("    PADDING-BOTTOM: 6px;");
txtstream.WriteLine("    COLOR: darkred;");
txtstream.WriteLine("    LINE-HEIGHT: 14px;");
txtstream.WriteLine("    PADDING-TOP: 6px;");
txtstream.WriteLine("    BORDER-BOTTOM: #999 1px solid;");
txtstream.WriteLine("    BACKGROUND-COLOR: #eeeeee;");
txtstream.WriteLine("    FONT-FAMILY: Cambria, serif;");
txtstream.WriteLine("    FONT-SIZE: 12px;");
txtstream.WriteLine("    text-align: left;");
txtstream.WriteLine("    white-Space: nowrap='nowrap';");
txtstream.WriteLine("}");
txtstream.WriteLine(".th");
txtstream.WriteLine("{");
txtstream.WriteLine("    BORDER-RIGHT: #999999 2px solid;");
txtstream.WriteLine("    PADDING-RIGHT: 6px;");
txtstream.WriteLine("    PADDING-LEFT: 6px;");
txtstream.WriteLine("    FONT-WEIGHT: Bold;");
txtstream.WriteLine("    PADDING-BOTTOM: 6px;");
txtstream.WriteLine("    COLOR: black;");
txtstream.WriteLine("    PADDING-TOP: 6px;");
```

```
txtstream.WriteLine("    BORDER-BOTTOM: #999 2px solid;");
txtstream.WriteLine("    BACKGROUND-COLOR: #eeeeee;");
txtstream.WriteLine("    FONT-FAMILY: Cambria, serif;");
txtstream.WriteLine("    FONT-SIZE: 10px;");
txtstream.WriteLine("    text-align: right;");
txtstream.WriteLine("    white-Space: nowrap='nowrap';");
txtstream.WriteLine("}");
txtstream.WriteLine("td");
txtstream.WriteLine("{");
txtstream.WriteLine("    BORDER-RIGHT: #999999 3px solid;");
txtstream.WriteLine("    PADDING-RIGHT: 6px;");
txtstream.WriteLine("    PADDING-LEFT: 6px;");
txtstream.WriteLine("    FONT-WEIGHT: Normal;");
txtstream.WriteLine("    PADDING-BOTTOM: 6px;");
txtstream.WriteLine("    COLOR: navy;");
txtstream.WriteLine("    LINE-HEIGHT: 14px;");
txtstream.WriteLine("    PADDING-TOP: 6px;");
txtstream.WriteLine("    BORDER-BOTTOM: #999 1px solid;");
txtstream.WriteLine("    BACKGROUND-COLOR: #eeeeee;");
txtstream.WriteLine("    FONT-FAMILY: Cambria, serif;");
txtstream.WriteLine("    FONT-SIZE: 12px;");
txtstream.WriteLine("    text-align: left;");
txtstream.WriteLine("    white-Space: nowrap='nowrap';");
txtstream.WriteLine("}");
txtstream.WriteLine("div");
txtstream.WriteLine("{");
txtstream.WriteLine("    BORDER-RIGHT: #999999 3px solid;");
txtstream.WriteLine("    PADDING-RIGHT: 6px;");
txtstream.WriteLine("    PADDING-LEFT: 6px;");
txtstream.WriteLine("    FONT-WEIGHT: Normal;");
txtstream.WriteLine("    PADDING-BOTTOM: 6px;");
txtstream.WriteLine("    COLOR: white;");
txtstream.WriteLine("    PADDING-TOP: 6px;");
txtstream.WriteLine("    BORDER-BOTTOM: #999 1px solid;");
txtstream.WriteLine("    BACKGROUND-COLOR: navy;");
txtstream.WriteLine("    FONT-FAMILY: Cambria, serif;");
txtstream.WriteLine("    FONT-SIZE: 10px;");
txtstream.WriteLine("    text-align: left;");
txtstream.WriteLine("    white-Space: nowrap='nowrap';");
txtstream.WriteLine("}");
txtstream.WriteLine("span");
txtstream.WriteLine("{");
txtstream.WriteLine("    BORDER-RIGHT: #999999 3px solid;");
txtstream.WriteLine("    PADDING-RIGHT: 3px;");
txtstream.WriteLine("    PADDING-LEFT: 3px;");
txtstream.WriteLine("    FONT-WEIGHT: Normal;");
txtstream.WriteLine("    PADDING-BOTTOM: 3px;");
txtstream.WriteLine("    COLOR: white;");
txtstream.WriteLine("    PADDING-TOP: 3px;");
txtstream.WriteLine("    BORDER-BOTTOM: #999 1px solid;");
```

```
txtstream.WriteLine("    BACKGROUND-COLOR: navy;");
txtstream.WriteLine("    FONT-FAMILY: Cambria, serif;");
txtstream.WriteLine("    FONT-SIZE: 10px;");
txtstream.WriteLine("    text-align: left;");
txtstream.WriteLine("    white-Space: nowrap='nowrap';");
txtstream.WriteLine("    display:inline-block;");
txtstream.WriteLine("    width: 100%;");
txtstream.WriteLine("}");
txtstream.WriteLine("textarea");
txtstream.WriteLine("{");
txtstream.WriteLine("    BORDER-RIGHT: #999999 3px solid;");
txtstream.WriteLine("    PADDING-RIGHT: 3px;");
txtstream.WriteLine("    PADDING-LEFT: 3px;");
txtstream.WriteLine("    FONT-WEIGHT: Normal;");
txtstream.WriteLine("    PADDING-BOTTOM: 3px;");
txtstream.WriteLine("    COLOR: white;");
txtstream.WriteLine("    PADDING-TOP: 3px;");
txtstream.WriteLine("    BORDER-BOTTOM: #999 1px solid;");
txtstream.WriteLine("    BACKGROUND-COLOR: navy;");
txtstream.WriteLine("    FONT-FAMILY: Cambria, serif;");
txtstream.WriteLine("    FONT-SIZE: 10px;");
txtstream.WriteLine("    text-align: left;");
txtstream.WriteLine("    white-Space: nowrap='nowrap';");
txtstream.WriteLine("    width: 100%;");
txtstream.WriteLine("}");
txtstream.WriteLine("select");
txtstream.WriteLine("{");
txtstream.WriteLine("    BORDER-RIGHT: #999999 3px solid;");
txtstream.WriteLine("    PADDING-RIGHT: 6px;");
txtstream.WriteLine("    PADDING-LEFT: 6px;");
txtstream.WriteLine("    FONT-WEIGHT: Normal;");
txtstream.WriteLine("    PADDING-BOTTOM: 6px;");
txtstream.WriteLine("    COLOR: white;");
txtstream.WriteLine("    PADDING-TOP: 6px;");
txtstream.WriteLine("    BORDER-BOTTOM: #999 1px solid;");
txtstream.WriteLine("    BACKGROUND-COLOR: navy;");
txtstream.WriteLine("    FONT-FAMILY: Cambria, serif;");
txtstream.WriteLine("    FONT-SIZE: 10px;");
txtstream.WriteLine("    text-align: left;");
txtstream.WriteLine("    white-Space: nowrap='nowrap';");
txtstream.WriteLine("    width: 100%;");
txtstream.WriteLine("}");
txtstream.WriteLine("input");
txtstream.WriteLine("{");
txtstream.WriteLine("    BORDER-RIGHT: #999999 3px solid;");
txtstream.WriteLine("    PADDING-RIGHT: 3px;");
txtstream.WriteLine("    PADDING-LEFT: 3px;");
txtstream.WriteLine("    FONT-WEIGHT: Bold;");
txtstream.WriteLine("    PADDING-BOTTOM: 3px;");
txtstream.WriteLine("    COLOR: white;");
```

```
txtstream.WriteLine("    PADDING-TOP: 3px;");
txtstream.WriteLine("    BORDER-BOTTOM: #999 1px solid;");
txtstream.WriteLine("    BACKGROUND-COLOR: navy;");
txtstream.WriteLine("    FONT-FAMILY:  Cambria, serif;");
txtstream.WriteLine("    FONT-SIZE: 12px;");
txtstream.WriteLine("    text-align: left;");
txtstream.WriteLine("    display:table-cell;");
txtstream.WriteLine("    white-Space: nowrap='nowrap';");
txtstream.WriteLine("    width: 100%;");
txtstream.WriteLine("}");
txtstream.WriteLine("h1 {");
txtstream.WriteLine("color: antiquewhite;");
txtstream.WriteLine("text-shadow: 1px 1px 1px black;");
txtstream.WriteLine("padding: 3px;");
txtstream.WriteLine("text-align: center;");
txtstream.WriteLine("box-shadow: inset 2px 2px 5px rgba(0,0,0,0.5), inset -2px -
2px 5px rgba(255,255,255,0.5);");
txtstream.WriteLine("}");
txtstream.WriteLine("</style>");
```

Shadow Box

```
txtstream.WriteLine("<style type='text/css'>");
txtstream.WriteLine("body");
txtstream.WriteLine("{");
txtstream.WriteLine("    PADDING-RIGHT: 0px;");
txtstream.WriteLine("    PADDING-LEFT: 0px;");
txtstream.WriteLine("    PADDING-BOTTOM: 0px;");
txtstream.WriteLine("    MARGIN: 0px;");
txtstream.WriteLine("    COLOR: #333;");
txtstream.WriteLine("    PADDING-TOP: 0px;");
txtstream.WriteLine("    FONT-FAMILY: verdana, arial, helvetica, sans-serif;");
txtstream.WriteLine("}");
txtstream.WriteLine("table");
txtstream.WriteLine("{");
txtstream.WriteLine("    BORDER-RIGHT: #999999 1px solid;");
txtstream.WriteLine("    PADDING-RIGHT: 1px;");
txtstream.WriteLine("    PADDING-LEFT: 1px;");
txtstream.WriteLine("    PADDING-BOTTOM: 1px;");
txtstream.WriteLine("    LINE-HEIGHT: 8px;");
txtstream.WriteLine("    PADDING-TOP: 1px;");
txtstream.WriteLine("    BORDER-BOTTOM: #999 1px solid;");
txtstream.WriteLine("    BACKGROUND-COLOR: #eeeeee;");
txtstream.WriteLine("
filter:progid:DXImageTransform.Microsoft.Shadow(color='silver', Direction=135,
Strength=16)");
txtstream.WriteLine("}");
txtstream.WriteLine("th");
txtstream.WriteLine("{");
```

```
txtstream.WriteLine("    BORDER-RIGHT: #999999 3px solid;");
txtstream.WriteLine("    PADDING-RIGHT: 6px;");
txtstream.WriteLine("    PADDING-LEFT: 6px;");
txtstream.WriteLine("    FONT-WEIGHT: Bold;");
txtstream.WriteLine("    FONT-SIZE: 14px;");
txtstream.WriteLine("    PADDING-BOTTOM: 6px;");
txtstream.WriteLine("    COLOR: darkred;");
txtstream.WriteLine("    LINE-HEIGHT: 14px;");
txtstream.WriteLine("    PADDING-TOP: 6px;");
txtstream.WriteLine("    BORDER-BOTTOM: #999 1px solid;");
txtstream.WriteLine("    BACKGROUND-COLOR: #eeeeee;");
txtstream.WriteLine("    FONT-FAMILY: Cambria, serif;");
txtstream.WriteLine("    FONT-SIZE: 12px;");
txtstream.WriteLine("    text-align: left;");
txtstream.WriteLine("    white-Space: nowrap='nowrap';");
txtstream.WriteLine("}");
txtstream.WriteLine(".th");
txtstream.WriteLine("{");
txtstream.WriteLine("    BORDER-RIGHT: #999999 2px solid;");
txtstream.WriteLine("    PADDING-RIGHT: 6px;");
txtstream.WriteLine("    PADDING-LEFT: 6px;");
txtstream.WriteLine("    FONT-WEIGHT: Bold;");
txtstream.WriteLine("    PADDING-BOTTOM: 6px;");
txtstream.WriteLine("    COLOR: black;");
txtstream.WriteLine("    PADDING-TOP: 6px;");
txtstream.WriteLine("    BORDER-BOTTOM: #999 2px solid;");
txtstream.WriteLine("    BACKGROUND-COLOR: #eeeeee;");
txtstream.WriteLine("    FONT-FAMILY: Cambria, serif;");
txtstream.WriteLine("    FONT-SIZE: 10px;");
txtstream.WriteLine("    text-align: right;");
txtstream.WriteLine("    white-Space: nowrap='nowrap';");
txtstream.WriteLine("}");
txtstream.WriteLine("td");
txtstream.WriteLine("{");
txtstream.WriteLine("    BORDER-RIGHT: #999999 3px solid;");
txtstream.WriteLine("    PADDING-RIGHT: 6px;");
txtstream.WriteLine("    PADDING-LEFT: 6px;");
txtstream.WriteLine("    FONT-WEIGHT: Normal;");
txtstream.WriteLine("    PADDING-BOTTOM: 6px;");
txtstream.WriteLine("    COLOR: navy;");
txtstream.WriteLine("    LINE-HEIGHT: 14px;");
txtstream.WriteLine("    PADDING-TOP: 6px;");
txtstream.WriteLine("    BORDER-BOTTOM: #999 1px solid;");
txtstream.WriteLine("    BACKGROUND-COLOR: #eeeeee;");
txtstream.WriteLine("    FONT-FAMILY: Cambria, serif;");
txtstream.WriteLine("    FONT-SIZE: 12px;");
txtstream.WriteLine("    text-align: left;");
txtstream.WriteLine("    white-Space: nowrap='nowrap';");
txtstream.WriteLine("}");
txtstream.WriteLine("div");
```

```
txtstream.WriteLine("{");
txtstream.WriteLine("    BORDER-RIGHT: #999999 3px solid;");
txtstream.WriteLine("    PADDING-RIGHT: 6px;");
txtstream.WriteLine("    PADDING-LEFT: 6px;");
txtstream.WriteLine("    FONT-WEIGHT: Normal;");
txtstream.WriteLine("    PADDING-BOTTOM: 6px;");
txtstream.WriteLine("    COLOR: white;");
txtstream.WriteLine("    PADDING-TOP: 6px;");
txtstream.WriteLine("    BORDER-BOTTOM: 999 1px solid;");
txtstream.WriteLine("    BACKGROUND-COLOR: navy;");
txtstream.WriteLine("    FONT-FAMILY: Cambria, serif;");
txtstream.WriteLine("    FONT-SIZE: 10px;");
txtstream.WriteLine("    text-align: left;");
txtstream.WriteLine("    white-Space: nowrap='nowrap';");
txtstream.WriteLine("}");
txtstream.WriteLine("span");
txtstream.WriteLine("{");
txtstream.WriteLine("    BORDER-RIGHT: #999999 3px solid;");
txtstream.WriteLine("    PADDING-RIGHT: 3px;");
txtstream.WriteLine("    PADDING-LEFT: 3px;");
txtstream.WriteLine("    FONT-WEIGHT: Normal;");
txtstream.WriteLine("    PADDING-BOTTOM: 3px;");
txtstream.WriteLine("    COLOR: white;");
txtstream.WriteLine("    PADDING-TOP: 3px;");
txtstream.WriteLine("    BORDER-BOTTOM: #999 1px solid;");
txtstream.WriteLine("    BACKGROUND-COLOR: navy;");
txtstream.WriteLine("    FONT-FAMILY: Cambria, serif;");
txtstream.WriteLine("    FONT-SIZE: 10px;");
txtstream.WriteLine("    text-align: left;");
txtstream.WriteLine("    white-Space: nowrap='nowrap';");
txtstream.WriteLine("    display: inline-block;");
txtstream.WriteLine("    width: 100%;");
txtstream.WriteLine("}");
txtstream.WriteLine("textarea");
txtstream.WriteLine("{");
txtstream.WriteLine("    BORDER-RIGHT: #999999 3px solid;");
txtstream.WriteLine("    PADDING-RIGHT: 3px;");
txtstream.WriteLine("    PADDING-LEFT: 3px;");
txtstream.WriteLine("    FONT-WEIGHT: Normal;");
txtstream.WriteLine("    PADDING-BOTTOM: 3px;");
txtstream.WriteLine("    COLOR: white;");
txtstream.WriteLine("    PADDING-TOP: 3px;");
txtstream.WriteLine("    BORDER-BOTTOM: #999 1px solid;");
txtstream.WriteLine("    BACKGROUND-COLOR: navy;");
txtstream.WriteLine("    FONT-FAMILY: Cambria, serif;");
txtstream.WriteLine("    FONT-SIZE: 10px;");
txtstream.WriteLine("    text-align: left;");
txtstream.WriteLine("    white-Space: nowrap='nowrap';");
txtstream.WriteLine("    width: 100%;");
txtstream.WriteLine("}");
```

```
txtstream.WriteLine("select");
txtstream.WriteLine("{");
txtstream.WriteLine("    BORDER-RIGHT: #999999 3px solid;");
txtstream.WriteLine("    PADDING-RIGHT: 6px;");
txtstream.WriteLine("    PADDING-LEFT: 6px;");
txtstream.WriteLine("    FONT-WEIGHT: Normal;");
txtstream.WriteLine("    PADDING-BOTTOM: 6px;");
txtstream.WriteLine("    COLOR: white;");
txtstream.WriteLine("    PADDING-TOP: 6px;");
txtstream.WriteLine("    BORDER-BOTTOM: #999 1px solid;");
txtstream.WriteLine("    BACKGROUND-COLOR: navy;");
txtstream.WriteLine("    FONT-FAMILY: Cambria, serif;");
txtstream.WriteLine("    FONT-SIZE: 10px;");
txtstream.WriteLine("    text-align: left;");
txtstream.WriteLine("    white-Space: nowrap='nowrap';");
txtstream.WriteLine("    width: 100%;");
txtstream.WriteLine("}");
txtstream.WriteLine("input");
txtstream.WriteLine("{");
txtstream.WriteLine("    BORDER-RIGHT: #999999 3px solid;");
txtstream.WriteLine("    PADDING-RIGHT: 3px;");
txtstream.WriteLine("    PADDING-LEFT: 3px;");
txtstream.WriteLine("    FONT-WEIGHT: Bold;");
txtstream.WriteLine("    PADDING-BOTTOM: 3px;");
txtstream.WriteLine("    COLOR: white;");
txtstream.WriteLine("    PADDING-TOP: 3px;");
txtstream.WriteLine("    BORDER-BOTTOM: #999 1px solid;");
txtstream.WriteLine("    BACKGROUND-COLOR: navy;");
txtstream.WriteLine("    FONT-FAMILY: Cambria, serif;");
txtstream.WriteLine("    FONT-SIZE: 12px;");
txtstream.WriteLine("    text-align: left;");
txtstream.WriteLine("    display: table-cell;");
txtstream.WriteLine("    white-Space: nowrap='nowrap';");
txtstream.WriteLine("    width: 100%;");
txtstream.WriteLine("}");
txtstream.WriteLine("h1 {");
txtstream.WriteLine("color: antiquewhite;");
txtstream.WriteLine("text-shadow: 1px 1px 1px black;");
txtstream.WriteLine("padding: 3px;");
txtstream.WriteLine("text-align: center;");
txtstream.WriteLine("box-shadow: inset 2px 2px 5px rgba(0,0,0,0.5), inset -2px -
2px 5px rgba(255,255,255,0.5);");
txtstream.WriteLine("}");
txtstream.WriteLine("</style>");
```